The San Francisco Poetry Renaissance, 1955–1960

Twayne's United States Authors Series

TUSAS 575

Philip Whalen, Anne Waldman, and Allen Ginsberg reading at Jack Kerouac School of Disembodied Poetics, Naropa Institute, Boulder, Colorado, summer 1975.
Courtesy of the photographer, Joel Scherzer, from *The Beat Diary* (1975) and *Look Quick 10* (Pueblo, Colorado, 1982).

The San Francisco Poetry Renaissance, 1955–1960

Warren French

D.H.L., Ohio University

Twayne Publishers
A Division of G. K. Hall & Co. • Boston

The San Francisco Poetry Renaissance, 1955–1960
Warren French

Copyright 1991 by G. K. Hall & Co.
All rights reserved.
Published by Twayne Publishers
A division of G. K. Hall & Co.
70 Lincoln Street
Boston, Massachusetts 02111

Copyediting supervised by Barbara Sutton.
Book production by Gabrielle B. McDonald.
Typeset in Garamond
by Compositors Corporation, Cedar Rapids, Iowa.

10 9 8 7 6 5 4 3 2 1

The paper used in this publication meets the minimum requirements
of American National Standard for Information Sciences—Permanence
of Paper for Printed Library Materials, ANSI Z39.48-1984. ∞™

Printed and bound in the United States of America.

Library of Congress Cataloging-in-Publication Data

French, Warren G., 1922-
    The San Francisco poetry renaissance, 1955-1960 / Warren French.
        p.   cm. — (Twayne's United States authors series ; TUSAS 575)
    Includes bibliographical references and index.
    ISBN 0-8057-7621-4
    1. American poetry—California—San Francisco—History and
criticism.   2. Beat generation—California—San Francisco.
3. American poetry—20th century—History and criticism.   4. San
Francisco (Calif.)—Intellectual life.   I. Title.   II. Series.
PS285.S3F74   1991
811'.540997946—dc20   90-46444
                                                              CIP

For Dick and Jeanne,
Mary Jeanne and Sally—my family
who saw me through
the Beat Generation
and other phenomena
of a disintegrating culture

Contents

Preface

This book is a work in progress, begun fifteen years ago. The roadblocks in its path were not only the exigencies of daily business as usual but, even more, the unexpected difficulties of researching recent events. One is not surprised that ephemera from Shakespeare's day are scarce; but one imagines that copies would have been preserved of a magazine, even a mimeographed one, that was the only collaborative venture of what Arthur Winfield Knight has justifiably called "the only serious literary movement indigenous to this country."[1] Yet I have not been able to examine a complete file of the first fifteen issues of *Beatitude,* the last transmissions of the San Francisco Poetry Renaissance in 1959 and 1960, nor any copies at all of *Underhound,* a North Beach beatnik newspaper of the same period.[2]

I have decided, however, that the time has come to publish the record that I have been able to assemble because recent events at the Naropa Institute in Boulder, Colorado, the last direct inheritor of the artifacts and spirit of this renaissance, will determine whether it continues to exert a generative force on a new generation or comes to rest in history, with other enkindling forces whose flames have been quenched. I hope that in transmitting this fragmentary account now I will elicit further information so that some day an expanded history of this unique episode in American cultural history can be written while some participants in the renaissance can still contribute.

Since key terms like "Beat," "Beat Generation," "beats and beatniks," "San Francisco Renaissance," and "San Francisco Poetry Renaissance" have been used indiscriminately and interchangeably for three decades, there is no generally agreed upon meaning for them. The Introduction will carefully define their usage in this study.

Thereafter, since this book is intended as a preliminary history, its progression will be roughly chronological. Chapter 1 expands the introductory details about the San Francisco Poetry Renaissance. After providing background material about members of the older San Francisco Renaissance and the Beat Generation, it carries the history forward to the reading at the Six Gallery on 7 October 1955 and the conclusion two years later of the *Howl* obscenity trial, which vindicated the poem and brought national attention to the San Francisco colony.

Chapter 2 starts by examining the responses to the renaissance between

1957 and 1959; that was a time when many prominently associated with the Beat Generation were traveling away from the city. Chapter 2 then focuses on the founding of *Beatitude* and its role for the next year in the community. Because of the unique importance of *Beatitude* as the only co-operative project of prominent beats, and because of its relative rarity today, Chapters 3 and 4 are devoted to a detailed analysis of the *Beatitude Anthology*, a collection of works chosen from its first fifteen issues by Lawrence Ferlinghetti. The anthology illustrates the two frequencies, "downbeat" and "upbeat," on which the beats broadcast.

Chapter 5 shows the influence of the North Beach community spreading up and down the California coast. Finally, Chapter 6 returns to look at what happened in San Francisco after 1960 and at the beat quest for a permanent home in Boulder, Colorado.

Some cautions are needed lest readers be disappointed by omissions from this chronicle. This is not another account of the misadventures of Burroughs, Ginsberg, and Kerouac in New York City in the 1940s, as a springboard for the beatnik antics of the 1950s. This book is part of a coordinated project, within the United States Authors Series, that seeks to provide a comprehensive portrayal of the beats' contribution to post–World War II American literature.

In the series, new studies of Robert Duncan—one of the founding leaders of the older San Francisco Renaissance—William Burroughs, and Jack Kerouac have joined earlier studies of Kenneth Rexroth and Gary Snyder and a revised version of Thomas F. Merrill's *Allen Ginsberg*. This book is being coordinated with another by Sy Kahn, a poet and theatrical director long connected with the University of the Pacific, on William Everson (known for a time as Brother Antoninus), Lawrence Ferlinghetti, and Charles Bukowski (a beat precursor, the entrepreneur who stabilized the beats, and a beat heir). These two books will provide a framework for the previous studies.

Because of its role in the larger project, this book scarcely mentions Everson or Burroughs (who never visited San Francisco during the poetry renaissance) and deals only in passing with Jack Kerouac and Allen Ginsberg, despite the central importance of *On the Road* and *Howl* to the development of the beat sensibility. The contributions of Kerouac and Ginsberg have already been dealt with at length in biographies and critical studies. Ferlinghetti's creative writings are also mentioned only in passing, and then only to stress how much his protégés owe to him. Ferlinghetti is that rarest of persons—a practical-minded, visionary businessman, without whom the most commendable experiments are likely to founder.

Originally I had intended to include in this book extensive studies of the writings of Gregory Corso, Michael McClure, and Philip Whalen, who many reviewers justly complain have been too much neglected, but such studies proved too long and digressive. They will require separate study, as will the subject of the activities generated by the beats outside California.

I have included accounts of the significant contributions made to the poetry renaissance and its aftermath by writers such as Bob Kaufman, Judson Crews, Pierre Henri DeLattre, and David Rafael Wang (the only native Asian contributor), as well as Lenore Kandel and other women writers whose work has not previously received the notice it deserves and who merit still further attention.

I regret that I have not been able to consult with surviving contributors to the San Francisco Poetry Renaissance to the extent that I hoped I might. But plentiful recollections are available, and my principal concern was to construct an outline of a history. I am deeply grateful to Roy Simmonds and Bob DeMott for providing me with essential needed materials, and especially to Ruth Nazum of Boulder for her encouraging response to my earlier books and a wealth of material about the Naropa Institute. I am also grateful to the courteous and knowledgeable staff at the John Hay Library at Brown University, where the Harris Collection of American Poetry and Plays boasts many unique materials, without access to which no history of this kind would be possible. I regret only that I was not able to make full use of its seemingly inexhaustible resources.

Much of this book derives, however, from beat memorabilia that I have been collecting since I met Evelyn Thorne and Will Tullos, editors of the avant-garde poetry magazine *Epos,* at Lake Como, Florida, in 1956. They supplied me with many copies of similar magazines publishing the beats that they exchanged with other editors. They also put me in touch with other sources that I might not otherwise have been able to locate before they disappeared. That this book exists is a tribute to their expertise, generosity, and dedication; the world sorely misses their like. My research has not been facilitated by support from any philanthropic sources ostensibly promoting scholarship.

I am greatly indebted to Thomas F. Merrill for a perceptive reading of my unedited text and his suggestions for extensive stylistic refinements, as well as to Arthur and Kit Knight for important corrections. I have been also greatly assisted and encouraged by Dave Moore, nonacademic editor of Britain's *The Kerouac Connection,* whose devotion to fostering the continuing recognition of beat writers and works has given me the impetus to go on with this work during my retirement overseas in the belief that the beat indeed goes on.

Chronology

1898   Lawrence Lipton born Lodz, Poland (date unknown).

1905   Kenneth Rexroth born South Bend, Indiana, 22 December.

1911   Kenneth Patchen born Niles, Ohio, 13 December.

1914   William Burroughs born, St. Louis, Missouri, 5 February.

1919   Robert Duncan born, Oakland, California, 7 January; Lawrence Ferlinghetti born Yonkers, New York, 24 March.

1920   Charles Bukowski born Andernach, Germany, 16 August.

1922   Jack Kerouac born Lowell, Massachusetts, 12 March.

1923   Carolyn Cassady born Lansing, Michigan, 28 April; Philip Whalen born Portland, Oregon, 20 October.

1925   Bob Kaufman born New Orleans, 18 April.

1926   Neal Cassady born Salt Lake City, 8 February; John Clellon Holmes born Holyoke, Massachusetts, 12 March; Allen Ginsberg born Newark, New Jersey, 3 June; Lew Welch born Phoenix, 16 August.

1927   Philip Lamantia born San Francisco, 23 October.

1928   Carl Solomon born Bronx, New York, 30 March.

1930   Gregory Corso born New York City, 28 March; Gary Snyder born San Francisco, 8 May; Pierre Henri DeLattre born Detroit, 2 July.

1932   Michael McClure born Marysville, Kansas, 20 October; Lenore Kandel born New York City; Jory Sherman born St. Paul, Minnesota, 20 October; David Rafael Wang born Hangchow, China.

1933   Peter Orlovsky born New York City, 8 July.

1934   Diane Di Prima born New York City, 6 August; Leroi Jones (Imamu Amiri Baraka) born Newark, New Jersey, 7 October.

1937   David Meltzer born Rochester, New York, 17 February.

1942   Duncan and Rexroth meet in San Francisco.

1944   Kerouac and Ginsberg meet in New York City and become friends of Burroughs.

1945   Anne Waldman born, Millville, New Jersey, 2 April.

1946 Neal Cassady arrives in New York from West Coast and asks Kerouac to teach him writing.

1947 Cassady, Ginsberg, and Kerouac spend summer in Denver; Kerouac's first visit to San Francisco.

1948 Jay Landesman founds *Neurotica* in St. Louis and on a talent-scouting trip to New York meets John Clellon Holmes; Holmes also meets Ginsberg and Kerouac the same weekend; Kerouac makes his first trip with Cassady.

1949 Ginsberg meets Carl Solomon at New York State Psychiatric Institute at Rockland; later, William Carlos Williams and Ginsberg meet in Passaic, New Jersey (the home town of both).

1950 Gary Snyder, Lew Welch, and Philip Whalen meet as students at Reed College, Portland, Oregon; Ginsberg and Kerouac meet Gregory Corso in New York.

1952 Holmes applies the term "Beat Generation" to Cassady and Kerouac in a *New York Times* article and in his novel *Go*.

1955 Lawrence Ferlinghetti begins City Lights Bookshop and City Lights Books; Corso's *The Vestal Lady on Brattle and Other Poems* is published; Ginsberg moves to Berkeley and meets Gary Snyder; reads first part of *Howl* 7 October at Six Gallery on a program with Philip Lamantia, Michael McClure, Gary Snyder, and Philip Whalen, with Kenneth Rexroth as master of ceremonies, marking the beginning of the San Francisco Poetry Renaissance.

1956 City Lights Books publishes *Howl and Other Poems*; Corso, Ginsberg, and Kerouac visit Mexico City; Gary Snyder goes to Japan.

1957 Kerouac's attempt to settle his mother in Berkeley fails before his *On the Road* is published in September. Ferlinghetti is prosecuted for selling "obscene material" (*Howl*) and exonerated by Judge Clayton Horn in October, while Ginsberg and Orlovsky are at the Beat Hotel in Paris.

1958 Neal Cassady begins two-year sentence at San Quentin for marijuana possession; Kerouac's *The Dharma Bums* and *The Subterraneans* are published; Ferlinghetti's *A Coney Island of the Mind* is published; Leroi Jones founds *Yugen* in New York; Feldman and Gartenberg's *The Beat Generation and the Angry Young Men* is published.

1959 Robert Frank films *Pull My Daisy* in New York; Albert Zugsmith films *The Beat Generation* in Hollywood; Allen Ginsberg records *Howl*; *Beatitude* is founded in San Francisco; *Big Table* is founded in Chicago; Lawrence Lipton's *The Holy Barbarians* is published.

1960 Donald Allen's *The New American Poetry* is published. *Beatitude* folds with closing of Pierre DeLattre's Bread and Wine Mission; Rexroth denounces commercializing of poetry; Ginsberg experiments with LSD with Timothy Leary; Kerouac has a nervous breakdown at Big Sur; Philip Whalen's *Like I Say* is published. Many beats move to Mexico.

1961 Kerouac's *Book of Dreams,* Ginsberg's *Kaddish and Other Poems,* and Thomas Parkinson's *A Casebook on the Beat* are published; "flower children" begin to create communes in Haight-Ashbury district of San Francisco.

1964 Kerouac and Cassady meet for the last time in New York at a party to celebrate publication of Ken Kesey's *Sometimes a Great Notion*; Gary Snyder returns from Japan to teach at Berkeley.

1965 Ginsberg is proclaimed King of May by students in Prague, then is expelled from Czechoslovakia for political activity; Kerouac's trip to France to recover his Breton roots is a disaster (described in *Satori in Paris*).

1966 Police take action in San Francisco against Lenore Kandel's *The Love Book*; police close down Michael McClure's play *The Beard*.

1968 Neal Cassady dies in Mexico; Diane Di Prima moves to San Francisco; Leroi Jones changes name to Imamu Amiri Baraka and becomes increasingly active politically.

1969 Jack Kerouac dies in St. Petersburg, Florida.

1974 "City Lights in North Dakota," Fifth Annual University of North Dakota Writers Conference, Grand Forks, 18–24 March; Chogyam Trungpa founds Naropa Institute in Boulder, Colorado.

1975 Ginsberg and Anne Waldman establish Jack Kerouac School of Disembodied Poetics at Naropa Institute at invitation of Trungpa.

1978 Joy Walsh begins publication of *Moody Street Irregulars.*

1982 Naropa conference to celebrate twenty-fifth anniversary of publication of *On the Road* is held in July; Kenneth Rexroth dies.

1984   Dave Moore founds *The Kerouac Connection* in Bristol, England; Corso, Ferlinghetti, and Ginsberg read at Poetry International in Albert Hall, London.

Introduction

The title of this book very specifically limits its topic. It is not an introductory history of the long-running San Francisco Renaissance, which took shape in 1944 with George Leite's publication of the first issue of *Circle* and which may still be in progress (though it has lost much of its momentum with the deaths of Kenneth Rexroth and Robert Duncan, who were its principal movers).[1] Nor is this book yet another repetition of the frequently told tale of what founders William Burroughs, Allen Ginsberg, and Jack Kerouac began calling the "Beat Generation" in New York City in the 1940s. Some mention of both phenomena will, of course, be necessary in this narrative.

What is here called the San Francisco Poetry Renaissance was associated in part with both of these larger movements, but it entirely encompassed neither and extended beyond both. The term is borrowed from Jack Kerouac's novel *The Dharma Bums* (1958), though I do not know whether he coined it, as he reputedly did "Beat Generation." Although it has not been universally used, it is useful in isolating and recounting a series of events that occurred in San Francisco between 1955 and 1960 and that have subsequently exercised a powerful influence on events elsewhere.

These events began on the night of Friday, 7 October 1955, with a poetry reading at the Six Gallery on Fillmore Street in the city's Marina District and ended in May 1960 when the last issue of *Beatitude* (pronounced *Beat-i-tude*) was distributed from Father Pierre Henri DeLattre's Bread and Wine Mission in North Beach, shortly before that beat refuge was closed.

The works that were produced and often performed in the area surrounding Chinatown during this period are usually lumped together as the work of the beats, though some of the writers involved rejected the label. Just who were these "beats"? The question is difficult to answer because, above all else, the beats disliked any form of organization or institutionalization; they issued no membership cards or manifestos, and they coyly or belligerently resisted efforts to collectivize or standardize them.

Serious attempts to define the term—and many other attempts to befuddle the idly curious—have been made by both insiders and outsiders, but there would be little point in reviewing them, since any attempt to narrate the history of such a phenomenon must settle upon one definition as a guiding principle, even if it is not received truth.

As often happens, a prominent figure associated with an elusive congregation will offer in the heat of confrontation an explanation that he or she would have avoided during more tranquil moments, which the beats especially sought to cultivate. Such a confrontation occurred when a lot of old-timers assembled at the Naropa Institute conference in Boulder, Colorado, in July 1982 to celebrate the twenty-fifth anniversary of the publication of Jack Kerouac's novel *On the Road*. Allen Ginsberg, whose first delivery of his poem *Howl* in 1955 is generally regarded as the kick-off of the poetry renaissance, provided a guide for interpreting its mission. He had been disturbed by earlier remarks by Abbie Hoffman, a by then somewhat subdued activist who had been leader of the late 1960s Yippie movement. (He had never actually been associated with the poetry renaissance.) Ginsberg said:

I think there was one slight shade of error in describing the Beat movement as primarily a protest movement, particularly Abbie. That was the thing that Kerouac was always complaining about; he felt the literary aspect or the spiritual aspect or the emotional aspect was not so much protest at all but a declaration of unconditioned mind beyond protest, beyond resentment, beyond loser, beyond *winner—way* beyond winner—beyond winner or loser, a declaration of unconditioned mind, a visionary declaration, a declaration of *unworldly love* that has *no hope* of the world and cannot change the world to its desire—that's William Carlos Williams—unworldly love, which means the basic nature of human minds, which is totally open, totally one with the space around, one with life and death. So, naturally, having that much insight, there'll be obvious smart remarks that might change society, as a side issue, but the basic theme was beyond the rights and wrongs of political protest.[2]

This is the concept that I will use in talking about what is called in the introduction to the *Beatitude Anthology*, "the beat frequency"—a metaphor chosen from radio technology to express the beats' mode of transmitting their messages.

Ginsberg's apparently impromptu eloquence poses problems—especially in grasping the meaning of the key term "unconditioned mind" as he used it to explain a vision "beyond protest"—because language itself, as has been urged tediously and tendentiously in recent years, is conditioned by teachings, traditions, prejudices, misunderstandings. Thus, the beats, trying to resist brainwashing, could express themselves only through a flawed medium that often made their vision incommunicable and certainly made it frequently misunderstood and irresponsibly condemned. Perhaps like the "unworldly love that has *no hope* of the world," the vision *is* beyond attainment; yet the beats believed that we must continue striving toward it, as the lack of it was responsible for the frightening perception Ginsberg expresses in the first line of *Howl*: "I saw the best minds of my generation destroyed by madness"—a madness engendered by the incessant pressure to condition minds into political, social, economic, religious, and ethnic conformity. Ginsberg locates the source of this pressure in special-interest groups that he tellingly identifies as "the three old shrews of fate the one eyed shrew of the heterosexual dollar the one eyed shrew that winks out of the womb and the one eyed shrew that does nothing but sit on her ass and snip the intellectual golden threads of the craftsman's loom."³

This concept of the "unconditioned mind," though the term may be new, is not itself new in American literature; it goes back to that first flowering of a native vision in the nineteenth-century transcendentalist movement. Although Ginsberg has acknowledged his affection for Whitman, the beats have said little about the wellsprings of their sensibility in Thoreau. Yet the kernel of Kerouac's complaint, as explained by Ginsberg, can be found in Thoreau's famous statement to the Concord selectmen: "Know all men by these presents, that I, Henry Thoreau, do not wish to be regarded as a member of any incorporated society which I have not joined" ("Civil Disobedience"). The beats took this sentiment one step further: they did not believe in joining *any*thing. Although Thoreau was most often inclined to be a "bad" citizen, he still wished to be a good neighbor. A century after his experiment at Walden Pond, neighborliness had virtually disappeared from the United States.

The beats' call for a transcendental openness to experience recalls Emerson's becoming "a transparent eyeball" ("Nature") and his American scholar's self-reliant rejection of conformity. But these parallels do not necessarily indicate a bookish indebtedness to Emerson; the beats discovered for themselves the original relation to the universe that Emerson recommended. The beats were also accused of fostering mindless conformity because of the antic behavior of the camp followers that San Francisco gossip columnist Herb Caen labeled "beatniks." It was the beatniks, not the productive poets, who the popular media sensationalized by stirring up an apathetic public with warnings of the dire threat they posed to the American way of life.

Like all camp followers of idealists who are *not* seeking to peddle panaceas, the beatniks were the worst thing that happened to the beats, and a distinction needs to be made between them. Thomas Parkinson observed, in the best account of the cult at the time it flourished, that "the beatnik is either not an artist or an incompetent and non-productive one." (He displays perhaps too much of his customary courtesy here; others took a harder line.) "The beat writer," he maintained, "on the other hand, is serious and ambitious. He is usually well-educated and always a student of his craft." Beats may, however, "use the beatnik milieu as their subject and their ideas and attitudes may be widely shared by current Bohemia."[4]

While beats generated beatniks, they were often (like Frankenstein) as terrified by their monstrous creations as were the "squares" of the 1950s. (Kerouac and Corso became especially virulent in their denunciations.)[5] One purpose of this history will be to downplay the overpublicized antics of the transient beatniks and to focus attention upon the work of those "serious and ambitious" artists who were championed by genuinely concerned avant-garde magazines and small publishing houses like Ferlinghetti's. (The most repugnant efforts to shock middle-class, suburban "squares" were kitschy films like Albert Zugsmith's *The Beat Generation* and Hollywood's trashing of Jack Kerouac's potboiler *The Subterraneans,* in which the novel's black female romantic lead was turned white.)

It should be apparent that I agree with the early (1957) judgment of William Hogan, book editor of the *San Francisco Chronicle,* that *Howl* was "the most significant long poem to be published in this country since World War II."[6] It is taking its place beside Walt Whitman's closely related "Song of Myself," which reached the public first exactly a century earlier (1855), and T. S. Eliot's *The Waste Land,* which though antipodal in many respects shares Ginsberg's view of the tragic consequences of a materialistic, mechanized, depersonalized culture and his hopes for transcending it.[7]

Nothing else that the beats—or any poets since—have written matches Ginsberg's inspirational breakthrough, but like *Leaves of Grass* and *The Waste Land, Howl* is not a monument that stands in splendid isolation. It generated the ferment that followed—the San Francisco Poetry Renaissance —and it is to tell that story, which has too often been lost or ignored, that I have written this book.

Chapter One
The Wild Beasts of North Beach

The San Francisco Poetry Renaissance was unlike similar awakenings—the first flowering of the Bay Area as a literary frontier in the days of Mark Twain and Bret Harte, the boisterous Chicago Renaissance of the early decades of the twentieth century, and the most successful, the Southern Renaissance in the Fugitive and Agrarian 1920s and 1930s—in that it was of short duration and can be dated with unusual precision.

No less an authority than Jack Kerouac informed us in *The Dharma Bums*—though he fictionalized the names of the participants to project his personal vision of them—that the poetry renaissance was born on the evening of the first reading of the first part of Allen Ginsberg's *Howl* (in the novel, Alvah Goldbook's *Wail*) at the city's Six Gallery (name retained in the novel). This was Friday evening, 7 October 1955. Incredibly, all five of the readers on that occasion remained among the best-known writers connected with the renaissance; besides Ginsberg, the readers were Philip Whalen and Gary Snyder, former roommates at Reed College in Portland, Oregon; Michael McClure, giving his first public reading; and Philip Lamantia, a surrealist who did not read his own work but that of a deceased friend, John Hoffman. The master of ceremonies was Kenneth Rexroth, the guiding force behind the older San Francisco Renaissance; Rexroth was the beats' first publicist, but he later broke with them when he thought that they had turned commercial. Kerouac, who served as the cheerleader, describes the event as a "mad night" during which he kept the audience of about seventy-five people mellow with red wine.[1]

The end came not quite five years later and involved basically the same group, though Rexroth had already disengaged himself and Gary Snyder was off in Japan. These restless travelers had often been on the road during the intervening years but most were back in the city, along with a beatnik crowd that they had attracted, in 1959 when, after a meeting in May, Allen Ginsberg, Bob Kaufman, and John Kelly began to publish from an office at 14 Bannam Alley near Chinatown's Grant Avenue a "weekly miscellany of poetry and other jazz designed to extol beauty and promote the beatific life among the various mendicants, neo-existentialists, christs, poets, painters, musicians and other inhabitants and observers of North

Beach, San Francisco, United States of America."[2] The publication was christened *Beatitude*. Even though it usually consisted of only twenty-one mimeographed, legal-size pages, the weekly schedule ultimately could not be maintained. But fifteen issues did emerge over the course of a year, the last eight from Father Pierre DeLattre's Bread and Wine Mission. From these Lawrence Ferlinghetti selected for the *Beatitude Anthology* poems and prose pieces by forty-one writers, "not all on the Beat frequency" and announced in a preface that the magazine would continue to "issue spasmodically from the underground caves of the City Lights bookstore." The next issue was produced in New York.[3] The title also continued to crop up from time to time on publications from various sources, though none were on the same "frequency."

As the original *Beatitude* was expiring, word about the beats (as differentiated from the beatniks) was just getting around. Events moved faster than America's circumspect book publishers could keep up with them.

During the 1950s the principal source of enlightenment for those interested in avant-garde writing was *New World Writing,* a semiannual paperback that was launched in April 1952 under the editorship of the dynamic Arabel J. Porter. Although the term "Beat Generation" had been known to cognoscenti since John Clellon Holmes's novel *Go* was published (also in 1952), many persons first encountered it in May 1957 when Kenneth Rexroth's essay "Disengagement: The Art of the Beat Generation" appeared in *New World Writing,* No. 11. He wrote about the poets who "have come up recently, like Lawrence Ferlinghetti, Allen Ginsberg, Gary Snyder, Philip Whalen, James Harmon [the little-known editor of the locally legendary 1947 *Ark*], Michael McClure. . . . [These poets] still have largely local reputations."[4]

The next year, 1958, Gene Feldman and Max Gartenberg's anthology *The Beat Generation and the Angry Young Men* linked the American and English rebel movements but had little to do with the San Francisco Poetry Renaissance. Only the original New York group—Burroughs, Ginsberg, Kerouac—were included, along with others like Chandler Brossard, who has denied any affinities with the beats. It also contained Rexroth's "Disengagement" essay, though by then he had already "disengaged" himself from his subject.

By the time Seymour Krim's self-promoting *The Beats* was published in March 1960—with his strident introductory claim that "what follows is strictly for now, today, this minute, this second"[5]—the poetry renaissance was winding down and many participants were leaving San Francisco, often for Mexico; Krim's collection turned out to be not a coming-out party but a

wake. When University of California professor Thomas Parkinson's perceptive and sympathetic *A Casebook on the Beat* was published in 1961, the
question posed by his essay "Phenomenon or Generation" had already been
answered: The San Francisco Poetry Renaissance had been like a skyrocket
that briefly illuminated the night in glowing colors and left a vivid impression upon the memories of its beholders. Its like was not to be seen again
soon. In San Francisco the action moved across town to the Haight-Ashbury
area, where the newly arrived "hippies" crowded Day-Glo poster stores and
forsook beat jazz for the blasting new sounds of rock.

A history of the poetry renaissance cannot be documented by the kind of
manifestos that the famous European avant-garde movements churned out;
one of the "literary, spiritual, emotional" aspects that brought the motley
company of beats together was a shared distrust of any kind of organized activity, formal association, or protocol. The history of this renaissance resembles most nearly that of the explosive and similarly short-lived assemblage
of painters who made France the center of a constantly changing, constantly
startling modern art between 1863 and 1924.

Les Fauves (Wild Beasts)

Indeed, the coming together of the Fauvist painters at Collioure[6] on
France's Mediterranean *Côte vermeille* exactly a half-century earlier resembles remarkably closely that of the beats at North Beach. (In fact, the label
"les fauves," which the art critic Louis Vauxcelles jokingly, but without hos-
tility, bestowed upon the French colorists, suited much better the habitués
of the North Beach coffeehouses.)[7] Although the outcomes of these two re-
generative alliances were to prove most dissimilar, the comparison with the
earlier phenomenon, which has been thoroughly studied, sheds light on the
later one, which has still been only dimly understood.

Both the fauves and the beats, their loose and fluctuating associations
based on a limited agenda, may be adequately represented in histories of
painting and literature by single characteristic works: Fauvism by, for example, André Derain's "Charing Cross Bridge" (1905), the transformation of
the usually unremarkable London cityscape characterized by monochro-
matic weather into an exploding rainbow of unadulterated colors of the
spectrum;[8] the Beat by Allen Ginsberg's *Howl* (complete with "Footnote"),
which plunges through the euphemisms that attenuate the material-
spiritual division in our predominantly money-changing society to protest
the way in which "the best minds" (spiritually and emotionally inspired) of a
generation have been "destroyed by madness." The beats, like the fauves,

were intent on breaking through gray reality to reveal humanity's obscured but luminous potential. Unlike the adherents of many intellectual and ideological movements, neither group sought to indoctrinate converts or to create elitist cabals for initiates; instead, both aimed to create liberating explosions, to blast away the moribund status quo's barriers to the sharing of inspired artistic visions.

Although both movements produced a startling and controversial impact and were short-lived, they were the products of long-smoldering forces. John Elderfield traced the emergence of Fauvism to twenty-two-year-old Henri Matisse quitting the "frustrating atmosphere" of Adolphe Bougureau's class at the Académie Julian (where San Francisco novelist Frank Norris had studied in the late 1880s) and in 1892 joining the studio of symbolist Gustave Moreau at the Ecole des Beaux-Arts; Moreau's painting was akin to the poetry of Arthur Rimbaud, who inspired Jack Kerouac (Elderfield, 17). Exactly fifty years later, in 1942, Kerouac quit the hothouse life of coach Lou Little's Columbia University football team when he realized that he wanted "to be a Beethoven instead of an athlete."[9] In 1898 Matisse was asked to leave Moreau's old studio, which since his death had been directed by the archconservative Fernand Cormon, and he enrolled at the Académie Carrière, where he would meet Derain around 1900 and other Fauves-to-be, such as Maurice Vlaminck in 1901. A half-century later, in 1948, Kerouac, after completing a traditional family history romance influenced by the work of Thomas Wolfe, took his first cross-country trip with Neal Cassady, which inspired him to begin work on an entirely new kind of spontaneous prose: the first versions of the novel that would subsequently be published as *On the Road* and that would find its final form in *Visions of Cody*.[10]

Matisse and his cohorts, although attacked by traditionalists, encountered less resistance during the early years of the century than Kerouac and Ginsberg would during the "silent generation" years of Sen. Joseph McCarthy's witch-hunts. Again, there was an exactly fifty-year separation between the fauves' inspiring summer of painting at Collioure in 1905 and the beats' reading at the Six Gallery in 1955, events that would establish both internationally as leaders of the avant-garde.

There is no need to attach an occult significance to these striking parallels. A particular affinity between the fauves and the beats is illustrated, however, by John Elderfield's explanation of the fauves: "Despite their circle of friendship and their generally similar styles, the Fauves were never a group linked by clearly defined ideological premises the way [others] were, nor did they seek to make any theoretical statement about their work, let alone produce a group manifesto, as did most subsequent modern movements" (40). But their most striking similarity is suggested by Elderfield's assertion that "although the Fauves were never a coherent, unified group, but a series of fluctuating constellations, they came temporarily to settle their orbits around Matisse, creating for a few brief years a dazzling combination of energy and color before dispersing to follow their own paths once again" (18).

Dazzling is the vital word here, and with *Ginsberg* substituted for *Matisse,* and *beats* for *fauves,* the sentence could scarcely be improved upon as a statement about the situation in a different art form a half-century later. And what term could better capture a sense of the poetry renaissance than "a series of fluctuating constellations"? What entitles the fauves to the small but significant space they occupy in the chronicles of painting is the immediacy of the impact of their works. To be confronted by the works of that magical summer of 1905 is not to be nostalgically transported back to Collioure but to participate in an experience that transcends time and space—to be plunged into the experience of "unconditioned mind" with the trappings that usually domesticate it stripped away. Elderfield precisely expressed this achievement in the introduction to his study: "The color and the brushwork of the Fauves possess a directness and individual clarity that even now can seem, if not raw, then declamatory, and of astonishing directness and purity" (13–14). It was the similarly "astonishing directness and purity" of Ginsberg's benediction to *Howl*—"Holy the supernatural extra brilliant intelligent kindness of the soul"—that astonished sympathizers and infuriated bigots.

As Elderfield explained, many of the cubist painters who would dominate the next great movement in modern art considered Fauvism "the last obstacle they had to overcome to create something that was entirely new" (141). The very disturbing difference between the influence of the fauves and the beats is that the fauves opened the door to new visions that kept painting a dynamic art until very recently, but no later movements have sustained the momentum that the beats generated.

The reason Fauvism was short-lived was explained by Georges Braque when asked why he abandoned it for cubism: "You can't remain forever in a state of paroxysm." Even Matisse agreed that each of the fauves later found some part of it excessive (Elderfield, 141). The loosely associated group began to break up by 1907, just after it had won its greatest recognition at the Paris Salon d'Automne in October 1906. Matisse and Derain, the leaders, were becoming dissatisfied with their work and were drifting apart. Similarly, the poetry renaissance showed signs of burning out before the verdict of the *Howl* obscenity trial, which vindicated not only the poem but the spirit of a renaissance that some critics were beginning to suggest had never existed. What paroxysmal vision had triumphed over the challenge of official censorship to its expression at this trial?

The Beat Begins Uncertainly

The *Howl* trial in 1957 was the confluence of two underground streams that had originated fifteen years earlier at opposite ends of the continent.

The story of the development of the Beat Generation in New York in the 1940s—and of its fictionalization, with great liberties, in Kerouac's early novel *The Town and the City* (1950) and, with disgruntled recollection, in his swan song, *Vanity of Duluoz* (1968)—has been told too often to need detailed recounting here.[11] But to set the scene for what would follow in California: Burroughs, Ginsberg, and Kerouac, all of whom were aspiring writers, met in New York City in 1944, when Kerouac and Ginsberg were students at Columbia College. Burroughs and Kerouac played around with a never published (probably never finished) novel, *And the Hippos Were Boiled in Their Tanks*. But nothing of literary consequence emerged from their decadent lifestyle until Neal Cassady arrived from Denver in 1946— when Kerouac was working on his first solo novel—and provided the impetus for the cross-country junkets memorialized in *On the Road*.

After spending the summer of 1947 in Denver with Ginsberg and Neal Cassady, who were then having an affair, Kerouac paid his first visit to San Francisco. But he apparently established no connections with the group of local poets that was developing around Kenneth Rexroth.

By 1948 Kerouac and Ginsberg were back together in New York, where they met John Clellon Holmes, another aspiring writer who fictionalized their relationships in his 1952 novel *Go,* which also included the first use in print of the term "Beat Generation." Holmes attributed the term to Kerouac by having Gene Pasternak, the character modeled on him, say, for example, of the character modeled on Neal Cassady, "It's been two weeks and I'll bet he hasn't even been looking [for work]. That's the *beat* generation for you."[12]

Meanwhile, sales of Kerouac's first novel had stopped after a few weeks, and when the new novel that would become *On the Road* was completed in 1951, no publisher was willing to take a chance on it. Another publisher dropped plans for a paperback edition of *Go* for fear of obscenity lawsuit. About the only encouragement the incipient beats received was from Jay

Irving Landesman, whom Holmes met the same weekend of 4 July 1948 that he met Ginsberg and Kerouac in New York.[13]

Because he suffered "a problem of identity," Landesman had launched with Louis Triefenbach in St. Louis an offbeat magazine, *Neurotica*.[14] Its affinity to the emerging beats is apparent from the editor's statement in the opening issue: "We are interested in exploring the creativeness of man who has been forced to live underground and yet lights an utter darkness with his muses, poetry, painting, and writing." *Neurotica* published Holmes's story "Tea for Two" in the second issue, and in the third, an essay in which, though Holmes never used the word *beat,* he described "a rebel without a cause," a figure that has become associated with the beats through Nicholas Ray's 1955 film of that name starring James Dean. Like *Howl,* the film, which achieved cult status with frustrated teenagers, attacked middle-class American smugness and apathy.[15] A more comprehensive conception of a member of the Beat Generation than the one ascribed to Kerouac's alter ego in *Go* is evoked by Holmes's description of the "rebel": "His distinctive characteristics are open darting eyes (to catch the latest artistic mutations), a flexible vocabulary (he was almost the first to use 'guilt,' 'neutron,' and 'real gone' as denotive symbolisms), and alternate expressions of complacency and desperation."[16] This figure, which could have been based on Kerouac, Holmes related to the turn-of-the-century decadent and the surrealist of the 1920s, "constantly collecting background material for some novel he will never write" (a comment that may have generated some of the tensions responsible for the unflattering portrait of Gene Pasternak in *Go*).

Neurotica was the outstanding harbinger of what would follow its demise in 1952. Its greatest service to the rising generation was its inclusion in the sixth issue of the first poem by Allen Ginsberg to appear outside a student publication. This bagatelle, "Pull My Daisy"—a series of injunctions, like the title one, that winds up with "raise my daisy up / Poke my paper / put my plum / let my gap be shut"—is a rollicking evocation of the gay face of the Beat. It subsequently inspired the movie of the same title that would be the crowning achievement of a much maligned movement and would celebrate its fundamental innocence and purity. (The movie is discussed in Chapter 6.)

Pre-beats

Neurotica also provided the springboard for perhaps the most outspoken of the pre-beats: the noisy performers who operated on the frequency the beats would preempt and who might have given new directions to bohemian America if brainwashed compatriots had not mistaken their messages for static. The man whom Jay Landesman credited with turning the magazine, "which started out as a joke," into one focusing on "a serious side of life"[17] was Gershon Legman, who contributed a series of articles that he had collected and published privately in 1949 as *Love and Death: A Study in Censorship* (a particularly troublesome problem for outspoken beats). Legman railed against "professional moral elements [who] believe that sex can be replaced by physical and emotional exertions measurably less violent than itself, such as calisthenics, cold baths, and bingo"; but he also argued that "religion suggests prayer. Psychiatry proposes sublimation. The man & woman in the street are interested in neither." "There is *no* mundane substitute for sex except sadism," he thunders.[18] For another nearly one hundred pages he makes a sweeping attack on the sadistic violence in popular murder mysteries and comic books, as well as on the hateful portrayal of women in fiction, from *Gone with the Wind* to what he considers the extreme example of Ernest Hemingway.

Legman's arguments foreshadowed the grounds for the successful attacks on literary and film censorship in the late 1950s and 1960s, but they came far ahead of their time. A timorous public was nervous about his controversial attacks on authoritarians who were making desperate efforts to maintain official censorship, particularly of sexual material. Legman, embittered and disgusted by Puritan prurience and effete youth, moved abroad to Volbonne, a cultural center near Cannes on Frances's Côte d'Azur, where he turned against those like the beats, whose "rebellion" he considered a fraud manipulated by the mass media. Legman was not a prophet of post–World War II "liberation" movements but an advocate of D. H. Lawrence's pre–World War I demands for sexual freedom. In *The Fake Revolt* (1967), which Legman distributed free from France, he expressed an outrage, by then shared by Jack Kerouac, that "the hippies, the cool-cats, the swingers, the beats the teeny-boppers already growing old (at seventeen), the psychedelic gang-bangers, crudwunkers, or whatever they will be told by the the the promoters to call themselves next year," were too irresponsible and gullible to sustain a serious revolutionary movement. "These are just the suckers or victims," he continued. "I would like to see some attention put to the people *behind* the beatniks for a change." Unfortunately, by the time of this outburst, the rebellious young were scoring successes, and he was far behind the times in his closing denunciation of "the Sexual Revolution's idea of sex" as "either something flagellational or coprophagous, or otherwise nauseatingly gimmicked up, or else [it] falls into the ultimate estrangements of the orgy ethic."[19] The word *beatnik* seemed already an evocation of something from the past, and the activists were concerned with something other than the perfect orgasm, whether conceived in Lawrentian or Reichian terms.

Much more important to the poetry renaissance than the cantankerously outdated Legman was a long-suffering poet and artist whom the beats attempted to honor—Kenneth Patchen. But Patchen, who had long suffered greatly from a serious back injury and would spend his last years in great pain, failed to reciprocate, probably in part because, although the first of his many important works, *The Journal of Albion Moonlight,* had appeared long before, in 1941, he had never received the kind of acclaim that the beats seemed to have received overnight. After the success of *Howl* and *On the Road,* Patchen issued a statement that repulsed the possibility of any rapprochement with the disappointed beats:

> What I have to say is said for the purpose of throwing light on a situation about which many people have expressed puzzlement.
>
> My name and activities have not figured in recent publication coverage of "the San Francisco Scene" for the simple reason that in so far as I could I rejected all such identification.
>
> I refused to be interviewed or photographed by *Life* magazine in connection with their story: I ignored all similar requests for material and the like from *The Evergreen Review, The Cambridge Review,* etc.
>
> Again, there is a simple, uncomplicated reason for this:
>
> I am not and never have been "a regional poet."
>
> Moreover, my participation in, and knowledge of, "the San Francisco Scene" is exactly zero.[20]

It is understandable that an intensely individualistic artist like Patchen, who had long struggled unsuccessfully to achieve recognition on his own, would resent and reject being publicized as part of the furor over some upstarts who had achieved local notoriety. His peevish statement, however, exhibits no real knowledge of or even interest in the beats. They certainly did not fancy themselves regional artists (most of them were not even from the region), but they did seek to give credit to the place that had first welcomed and supported, even inspired them in creating works that received national and international attention.

Patchen's devoted wife, Miriam, proved more willing to cooperate when the beats lost regional identification after the fading away of the poetry renaissance. After *The Outsider* (a New Orleans publication discussed in Chapter 6) ran some excellent reproductions of Patchen's drawings, along with an appeal for his surgery fund, and then dedicated its third issue to him,

Miriam Patchen wrote editors Gypsy Lou and Jon Edgar Webb letters for publication about the increasingly desperate state of his health in 1962.

After Patchen's death in 1972, she attended the 1974 University of North Dakota writers conference, "City Lights in North Dakota," which included a large exhibit of Patchen's art. In a group photograph she stands amid but aloof from an otherwise all-male group—a small, determined woman who has obviously suffered greatly.[21] It is regrettable that the long-suffering Patchen could not come to some understanding with the beats; he appears to have been one of those individuals who are so insistent upon their autonomy that they create barriers that undermine their chances of achieving recognition.

The beats were on considerably better terms with the nearly mythical figure they regarded as a kind of patron saint, Henry Miller. Grove Press even prevailed upon Miller to provide a preface for Kerouac's novel *The Subterraneans*; the garrulous raconteur rambled on in his customary fashion about Kerouac's having "done something to our immaculate prose from which it may never recover"; Kerouac had taken "pleasure in denying the laws and conventions of literary expression which cripple genuine, untrammeled communication between reader and writer."[22] Although Miller was living nearby at Big Sur during the poetry renaissance, he had few actual meetings with the beats during those years. (Kerouac's novel *Big Sur* contains a fictionalization of his and Neal Cassady's ludicrous attempt to visit Miller in 1960.)

Actually, the beats were closer to the Miller of *The Air-Conditioned Nightmare* (1945)—a rambling attack on American bourgeois consumer culture, a subject that Ginsberg handled better in *The Fall of America* (1972)—than to the more celebrated Miller of the early *Tropics* (Cancer and Capricorn), which mixed shameless libertinism with page after page of blowsy philosophizing based on D. H. Lawrence, Nietzsche, and astrology. During the years of the poetry renaissance, however, Miller did not cultivate a beat image because he and his New York publisher were trying to sanitize his prose and fashion for him a respectably pathetic image—following the model of Chaplin's tramp in his early comedies and resembling the "little man" to come in Woody Allen's farces from 1968 to 1977.[23] This effort had begun back in 1948 with *The Smile at the Foot of the Ladder*, a tragic clown story that Kingsley Widmer considers Miller's most maudlin book.[24] The effort to cast Miller as the champion of a free speech movement did not begin until Grove Press made its boldest and most costly attack on American literary censorship with its first publication in this country, in 1960, of *Tropic of Cancer*, originally published in Paris in 1934.

Both Miller and Gershon Legman, who shared his Edwardian conceptions of sexual abandon, would probably have been happier to see what Henry Luce's *Life* called in 1959 "the only rebellion around" in the hands not of the beat but of Judson Crews—if they had happened to be familiar with his obscure works. Crews was identified by *The Outsider* as a writer who had been published "repeatedly for years in many of the little magazines and will continue to be."[25] Crews did continue to play the bush circuit and never hit the big time. He is of more than passing interest, however, as possibly the most prolific of those "outsiders" whose work won its way into avant-garde poetry journals but who never managed, like Charles Bukowski, to break through into better-paying publications. He is a somewhat mysterious figure, largely because no one has tried to disinter his history. He operated out of D. H. Lawrence's last resort, Taos, New Mexico, where in 1950–51 he produced five issues of the bizarrely titled *Suck-Egg Mule*. Apparently temporarily embarrassed for funds, he contributed extensively to other exotic organs until the late 1950s, when he edited eleven issues of the beat-oriented *Naked Ear*.

The reason Crews encountered difficulties with commercial publishers is suggested by his contribution to *The Outsider:* two poems on his perennial subject, the shorter of which is titled "Pastoral":

> The furrow opening out, cool
> warming in the sun
> receiving seed, covered
>
> Oh lovely body, yours.[26]

What particularly mystified those browsers in the largely closed gardens of avant-garde poetry journals was the identity of Crews's protégé, Mason Jordan Mason, whose work appeared almost as frequently as Crews's and always in similar contexts. Crews identified Mason only vaguely as a promising young black poet (at a time when black contributions to such journals were rare); but no one else ever reported meeting Mason, and his picture never appeared with his works. He was reportedly traveling in distant places. His works, however, were often written in a putative black dialect that resembled that of minstrel-show jokes, which black poets of the period like Langston Hughes would have spurned. Mason's subject matter was also invariably the same as Crews's. Both characteristics of his alleged work are illustrated in *The Outsider* by some lines from "Mysterious as Any Woman Be":

. . . a fast high yellow
keep a pretty sharp blade

And the sorrow she feel
is purchased away
when she cut off his pleasure

But somehow
she seem just a little bit
sad all the same.[27]

Suspicions began to develop that Mason was a name for an alter ego that Crews had created, and occasionally editors apparently in on the secret dropped hints to this effect. It might be interesting to know Crews's motives if he were masquerading as a black; but nevertheless, the two personalities wrote remarkably similar verse on a narrowly limited subject.

The probable reason for the failure of both Crews/Mason to place poems in widely circulated journals was a fear, justified by the censorship of *Howl* and *Tropic of Cancer,* that such explicitly sexual material would be suppressed. (Avant-garde poetry journals, on the other hand, rarely strayed into the wrong hands.) Crews/Mason was certainly producing the kind of work that Legman and Miller were calling for, but such work was distinctly not on the beat frequency. Crews and Mason, along with others, were producing an alternative poetry—old-fashioned in a nuclear age—that might have earlier enjoyed the celebrity that the beats' poetry eventually did if the temper of the times and the complacent American status quo had been different.

Their obscurity, however, helps explain why, as the outraged Legman saw things, "the right to publish openly *Lady Chatterley's Lover* and Lawrence's apotheosis of orgasm BECAUSE THEY ARE SOCIALLY VALUABLE, has become instead the pretext for swamping and overwhelming sexual normality in print and in life with a type of perverted stuff."[28] The beats were not especially concerned with winning freedom for the open and unlimited discussion of heterosexual intercourse. Despite some lurid journalistic revelations about beatnik orgies, the poetry renaissance was not primarily interested in the artistic glorification of sex at all. Consistent with the Buddhist tendencies of some of the most respected beats, the concern was not with the lifting of bans against many forms of sexual expression but with spiritual regeneration. The beats were not primarily attacking frustrating Puritanism but brainwashing materialism. Although there are exceptions, most beat poetry is not erotic; and most of the traditional heterosexual romantic poetry in *Beatitude* is by female contributors.

In fact, those associated with the beats did not face a censorship challenge involving material that Legman would have regarded as dealing with "sexual normality" until 1966, when Lenore Kandel's *The Love Book* was challenged and exonerated. Kandel had begun publishing with the beats during the poetry renaissance, but *The Love Book* appeared much later in a vastly altered milieu in which spiritual quests had been subordinated to an activist campaign for individuals' right of choice. Crews's poetry might have found a more responsive audience at that time, but little was heard from him in the 1960s. He was not among the many old contributors to appear again in the last issue of *The Outsider* in 1969. In 1982, however, he did send a poem from Las Cruces, New Mexico, to *Look Quick 10* in Pueblo, Colorado. He could yet be discovered as a cult figure, but his example is probably most useful in reminding us that the beats were not "the only rebellion around" in the 1950s but the one that respectable tastemakers thought the most threatening.

Six Gallery, San Francisco, 7 October 1955

Even that threat caused little concern until October 1955. When the seventh issue of *New World Writing* in 1955 led off with Jack Kerouac's "Jazz of the Beat Generation," there was no indication that this "generation" might produce the nation's most important new poetry since World War II. Ironically, this very issue concluded with Donald Hall's long contemplation, "The New Poetry: Notes on the Past Fifteen Years," which did not mention the beats at all and evoked the San Francisco Renaissance only in one condescending comment: Hall was "not sure that closeness to common speech is a test of the worth of poetry," but he felt that "the deadness of anarchist verse like Kenneth Rexroth's" seems "far from common speech."[29] The poetry that Hall deemed worthy of survival was most of Robert Lowell's and the best of Richard Wilbur, Theodore Roethke, J. V. Cunningham, and Karl Shapiro. Rexroth would get revenge with the publication of "Disengagement: The Art of the Beat Generation" in *New World Writing* 11 in May 1957; but in between Donald Hall's shortchanging of the Bay Area and Rexroth's pronouncements, Ginsberg had written *Howl* and read the first part of it that October night at the Six Gallery, and San Francisco was on its way to becoming the center of the national poetry "scene" for the last years of the decade.

Several accounts of this event have been preserved, from which some approximation of the progress of the evening can be pieced together.[30] Ginsberg described the venue as "a run down secondrate experimental art gallery in the Negro section of San Francisco," but Michael McClure recalled it more fondly as a cooperative art gallery run by young artists involved with the San Francisco Art Institute—"a huge room that had been converted from an automobile repair shop." Ginsberg reported that a hundred postcards had been sent out publicizing the event,[31] and McClure estimated that "a hundred and fifty enthusiastic people had come to hear us."

The program opened with Philip Lamantia reading not his own poems but some by his dead friend John Hoffman. (Renaming him Altman, Kerouac reported that he had died from eating "too much peyote in Chihuahua [or died of polio, one].") McClure described the works as "beautiful prose poems that left orange stripes and coloured visions in the air." McClure himself, the youngest of the group reading (twenty-three later that month), read next; according to Ginsberg, he represented the "Black Mountain group," and besides his own poems, he read some of Robert Duncan's.

Kerouac made no comment about McClure's performance, but the poet himself identified the poems he read as "Point Lobos: Animism," "Night Words: The Ravishing," "Poem"—beginning, "Linked part to part, toe to knee, eye to thumb . . ."—and "For the Death of 100 Whales," commenting later, "I did not fear obscurity in my poetry because I had come to believe that the way to the universal was by means of the most intensely personal. . . . Communication to me is not as important as expression. To speak and move was the most important thing." He emphasized in his recollections of the event his "horrified and angry" response to an article in *Time* about the slaughter of whales, which he thought could only have been portrayed in Goya's *Horrors of War* series.

The feature of the evening was probably expected to be the reading by Philip Whalen, already familiar to the audience. Ginsberg described Whalen at that time as "a strange fat young man from Oregon," obviously careless of his reputation as a poet, and Kerouac called him "a big fat bespectacled quiet booboo," whom he found "too incomprehensible to understand." (Another Kerouac remark about finding another of the readers "too political" could apply only to McClure, who always kept much more in touch with what was going on around him than Kerouac.) McClure later wrote admiringly of Whalen's reading of "Plus ça change," as the meaning of this "metaphoric poem gradually began to sink in." He found that Whalen was using "American speech for the naked joy of portraying metamorphosis and of exemplifying and aiding change in the universe"; Whalen read the poem "with a mock seriousness that was at once biting, casual, and good natured."

The tone changed dramatically when Ginsberg, in his own words, provided "the most brilliant shock of the evening" with his "declamation" of *Howl.* He added that he was "rather surprised at his own power, drunk on the platform, becoming increasingly sober as he read, driving forward with a strange ecstatic intensity, delivering a spiritual confession to an astounded audience—ending in tears which restored to American poetry the prophetic consciousness it had lost since the conclusion of Hart Crane's *The Bridge,* another celebrated mystical work."

Kerouac mentioned only that by 11:00 P.M., when Ginsberg read, "everybody was yelling 'Go! Go! Go!' (like a jam session) and old Rheinhold Cacoethes [Rexroth] the father of the Frisco poetry scene was wiping his tears in gladness." McClure recalled that it was Kerouac "who began shouting 'Go' in cadence as Allen read"; he then provided the highest praise of Ginsberg's performance: "In all of our memories no one had been so outspoken in poetry before—we had gone beyond the point of no return—and we were ready for it, for a point of no return. None of us wanted to go back to the gray, chill, militaristic silence, to the intellectual void—to the land without poetry—to the spiritual drabness."

One would have supposed that after this scene (Ginsberg read only the first part of the poem—the rest was not finished), anything more would have been anticlimactic, but Ginsberg himself graciously acknowledged that "the last poet on the platform was perhaps more remarkable than any of the others." Gary Synder, also new to the crowd, read from *Myths and Texts,* which Ginsberg described as "fragments of all his experiences forming an anarchic and mystical pattern of individual revelation." Kerouac was also carried away by Snyder's knowledge of Oriental culture and American barroom humor, and by the way his "deep and resonant and sometimes brave" voice, like those of "oldtime American heroes and orators," projected his "anarchistic ideas about how Americans don't know how to live." McClure was less captivated, though he wrote a touching appreciation of the "bearded and neat" Snyder's "scholarly and ebullient" nature poem, "A Berry Feast," in which he hears "concern" that we must "step outside of the disaster that we have wreaked upon the environment and upon our phylogenetic selves."[32] The immediate triumph, however, was Ginsberg's. Ferlinghetti sent him a telegram echoing Emerson's letter to Whitman after reading the first edition of *Leaves of Grass:* "I greet you at the beginning of a great career. When do I get the manuscript?"[33]

The evening must have been an occasion without parallel in the history of

American literature. But *Howl* did not become a national sensation over-night; Ginsberg had the final strophes and the "Footnote" to finish, and Ferlinghetti could not rush publication. In those days it was cheaper to send typescripts to England—where Villiers Publications in Holloway (London) specialized in avant-garde works—and to have the printed sheets returned to the United States. As a result, *Howl* was not available in print until October 1956, a year after its first performance, and a month after the first enthusiastic report about the Pacific Coast upstarts by a respected member of the East Coast coterie, Richard Eberhart, appeared in the *New York Times Book Review* on 2 September. Even then it was not a sellout; a second printing from England was not required for six months—not until April 1957—though even the need for a reprinting was an indication of unusual popularity, since few volumes of poetry required a second issue. Through 1956 the beats remained only local celebrities.

The San Francisco Renaissance

During 1956 there had also been a falling out between the emergent beats and the grand panjandrum of the Bay Area scene, Kenneth Rexroth, who had enthusiastically emceed the 1955 reading. Tom Clark's explana-tion of this estrangement was that "the very success of Allen's reading . . . caused an immediate division in the 'Renaissance,' by challenging the local preeminence of Rexroth as a poet." Then Robert Creeley, who had become a close friend of Kerouac's, fell in love with Rexroth's wife: "When Kenneth went out of town, Bob took Jack along on a visit to the Rexroth flat. When Rexroth returned, he presumed Jack's 'complicity' in adultery. . . . Then Ginsberg's scheme to build a 'united front' of East and West Coast poets caused jealousies to run rife over who were the *real* 'San Francisco poets,' now that the *New York Times* had written about them and *Mademoiselle* was coming to town to take their pictures."[34] (*Mademoiselle*'s arrival on this tense scene caused particular pique against the beats on both coasts, pique that can only be attributed to the jealousy of those not similarly honored.)

Longtime residence and seniority were important to San Francisco's fas-tidious anarchists, who were beginning to resent the upstarts from the East. (Tom Clark reported that not long after the reading at the Six Gallery, at one of "Rexroth's regular Friday afternoon 'at-homes,' Kerouac and Ginsberg were drunk" and Ginsberg "boastfully inform[ed] his host, 'I'm a better poet than you are.' ")[35] As Thomas Parkinson points out in *A Casebook on the Beat*, "From about 1944 on, the area had been distin-guished by considerable artistic activity, and during that period it was one of the strongholds of experimental poetry" (281). As a literary frontier, the city had posed a challenge to the Northeast since 1866 when Mark Twain and Bret Harte established a particularly Western literary tradition, especially through the *Overland Monthly,* published from 1868 to 1875 (although by 1875 Twain had already decamped to the East and Harte was preparing to spend the rest of his life in Europe).

A San Francisco renaissance at the end of the nineteenth century—which began with the founding of the sprightly magazine *The Lark* by "les jeunes," led by humorist Gelett Burgess and then continued through the success of novelists Gertrude Atherton, Jack London, and Frank Norris—was cut short by Norris's early death in 1902 and the earthquake of 1906. The painfully rebuilt city turned increasingly conservative and became the commercial capital of the West Coast. From World War I to the end of World War II, it was overshadowed artistically by southern California's more glamorous film capital, Los Angeles, which attracted international celebrities such as Aldous Huxley, Thomas Mann, and film directors Fritz Lang and Jean Renoir (not all of whom were particularly happy there). San Francisco missed a golden opportunity by largely ignoring northern California's native son, John Steinbeck—who eventually won a Nobel Prize for Literature—particularly when the international success of his novel *The Grapes of Wrath* (1939) was coinciding with the city's bid for recognition as an international trade center with its ultraconservative Golden Gate International Exposition. Steinbeck followed the earlier example of Twain and Frank Norris in moving east.

But a determined few who enjoyed the city's natural beauty and mellow climate pushed to restore its stature as a cultural center, despite the region's enervating anti-intellectualism and its financial leaders' reluctance to subsidize possibly subversive literary activities. The spark plug of the movement was Rexroth, a Midwesterner who as a teenager participated in the Chicago Renaissance, then moved at twenty-two to San Francisco to become involved in leftist politics. He wrote poems in the tradition of Edwin Markham, whose "The Toilers" had inspired Frank Norris in *The Octopus.* In 1940 Rexroth's first collection, *In What Hour,* won the California Literature Silver Medal Award; in 1941 he declared himself a conscientious objector, and in 1942 he met Robert Duncan, who had received a psychological discharge from the army. Duncan did not remain on the West Coast but returned in 1946 to study medieval and renaissance civilization at the University of California at Berkeley under Ernst Kantorowicz. In the meantime, in 1944, George Leite had founded in Berkeley the literary and political journal *Circle,* which reflected the pacifist and anarchist tendencies of its contributors. The magazine continued through ten issues until 1948 and featured not only local contributors like Duncan but also Henry Miller and poet Josephine Miles of the Berkeley faculty.

Duncan was principally responsible for fostering public poetry readings, and this enterprise received a great boost in 1949 when the Pacifica Foundation (named not for the neighboring ocean but for the group's pacifist tendencies) launched radio station KPFA on the newly available FM band (which it was expected would provide more local public-service broadcasts because of its limited effective radiation area and its static-free reception, in contrast to the heavily commercial AM band).[36]

The renaissance, whose participants were constantly harassed by suspicious neo-Fascist groups during the years of Richard Nixon's witch-hunts, did not take another important step forward until 1954, when the downfall of Sen. Joseph McCarthy considerably cleared the air. Then Ruth Witt-Diamant opened the Poetry Center at San Francisco State College (now University) to provide a platform for aspiring locals and distinguished visitors.

Interest in such readings had been greatly stimulated by the lamentable death in 1953 of Dylan Thomas, the Welsh bard whose programs of readings from his own lyrics and works of other poets had restored poetry to its honored place as a performing art. Thomas's American tours during his last years had engendered enthusiasm akin to that for the next decade's rock concerts, and his legend inspired the San Franciscans. Kenneth Rexroth wrote one of the most powerful elegies in Thomas's memory, "Thou Shalt Not Kill," which bristles with lines like "Henry Luce killed him with a telegram to the Pope."[37]

Parkinson was thus justified in his insistence that when the beats arrived in San Francisco, "they were not entering a cultural void"; rather, "they found a sounding board. . . . The audience and the structure of public address were there, and the literary atmosphere was receptive. . . . They were supported by an environment that, in turn, they changed" (285).[38]

Parkinson also emanated a gracious appreciation missing in many accounts of the beats. In his tribute to Ginsberg's role "in revivifying the poetic life of the Bay area," he maintained that "too little stressed in all the public talk about Ginsberg are his personal sweetness and gentleness of disposition. He was a person more cohesive than disruptive in impact" (285). The tone of Parkinson's whole unparalleled review of the San Francisco poetry scene in the decade between Robert Duncan's return to the city and Ginsberg's first reading conveyed the impression that, before the appearance of the beats, the participants in the San Francisco Renaissance were too genteelly inclined to desire any vulgar success. This impression is strengthened by Mark Andrew Johnson's description of "The Maidens," a group that gathered to read poems and plays in the 1950s and that included Duncan, filmmaker James Broughton, Eve Triem, Madeleine Gleason, and Helen Adam, who was "sometimes deliberately childish."[39] Certainly Michael Davidson's illumination of the "gnostic poetics" of Jack Spicer—a longtime associate of Duncan, a close friend of Thomas Parkinson, and an influential member of the San Francisco Poetry Workshop group—shows how much Spicer's work differed from that of the beats: "The poem is regarded as a mysterious code or message coming from an outside voice. Unlike the poetry of the Beats, this verse does not originate from within the artist's expressive will as a spontaneous gesture unmediated by formal constraints. . . . Poetry is a foreign agent, a parasite that invades the poet's language and expresses what 'it' wants to say. The poet's task, then, is to clear away the intrusive, authorial will and allow entrance to an alien and ghostlike language."[40] This extraordinarily revealing account identifies the poet as a transmitter, like the one in Cocteau's play and film *Orpheus,* and as a practitioner of a kind of orphism that can be traced back to the Eleusinian mysteries of ancient Greece—though it is probably far older—and that continues to turn up regularly. Bronson Alcott tried to revive it with a conspicuous lack of success during the transcendentalist days in Concord; and it has persisted, through many transformations, in the trances of Madame Blavatsky, the automatic writing of Gertrude Stein, and the ouija board transcriptions of James Merrill. This concept of poetry as a message from "beyond" to be received mediumistically is just the one that Ginsberg shook himself free from in 1963 with "The Change: Kyoto-Tokyo Express." It appears to have influenced the work of Philip Lamantia, however, who despite his affinity for the beats resisted identification with them.

Ginsberg, despite his longings for Blakean visions, had broken loose in *Howl* from this fatalistic concept of the artist as a tool in the hands of mysterious powers. *Howl* is firmly grounded in an outraged perception of the concrete details of contemporary reality. This perception was to prove too much for mandarin San Francisco to tolerate without a struggle.

San Francisco Scene, 1957: The Stock Report

Whatever else may have been going on in San Francisco, on the poetry front the new year of 1957 probably dawned as serenely as it had hours earlier in Collioure, fifty years after the departure of the fauves. The fomenters of beat activity were not in town: Kerouac was in New York, preparing to sail for Tangier to visit Burroughs; Ginsberg, who had lured Kerouac back to New York, was preparing to join them, along with Gregory Corso; Gary Snyder was in Asia; only Whalen and McClure were in town, but they were longtime residents and neither had yet published a disturbing book. It seemed entirely possible that any aftereffects of that overheated evening back in 1955 might have been dissipated, and that the Beat Generation would have amounted to no more than a quickly burst bubble in the unglamorous history of San Francisco's attempt to rustle up a renaissance. At least, so it seemed to one commentator who had recently returned from Brazil to provide a detailed account of the poetic scene in San Francisco.

Poetry Broadside was yet another short-lived effort to provide an inexpensive bulletin board for young poets. It was edited by Barbara Romney with an all-woman staff on New York's then somewhat rundown West Side near 93d Street and Columbus Avenue. It first appeared in April 1957 (just after the U.S. Customs Office in San Francisco had seized part of the second printing of *Howl*) with the blessing of Alan Swallow, the most generous and dedicated of American avant-garde publishers. From his home in Denver, Swallow kept in print works that he believed in even if the world did not (the novels of Anaïs Nin, for example), and he contributed to the first issue of *Poetry Broadside* an article on the difficulty of publishing poetry in the United States. That issue also carried a letter from London commenting on the continuing influence of Dylan Thomas as part of a "demoniac" school of poetry flourishing there.

In the second issue that summer a "Letter from San Francisco" was added. It was written by Robert Stock, who was a thirty-four-year-old contemporary of Philip Whalen and, with James Harmon, a coeditor of *The Ark,* a legendary anarchist poetry anthology published ten years before. Stock had recently spent four years in Brazil and had therefore missed the action in San Francisco during the mid-1950s. Back in the city, he was working on translations of Brazilian poets.

The tabloid newspaper format of *Poetry Broadside* provided more space than was usually available to financially straitened poetry journal publishers. There was plenty of room for a long rambling letter that provided a uniquely comprehensive if highly biased picture of the San Francisco scene—from the break between Rexroth and the beats to the action against *Howl,* which Stock did not mention. (The letter was not dated, so that although it was intended for the summer issue, it had probably been written during the lull before the stormy disputes over Ginsberg's poem).

Stock began by attributing "San Francisco's recurrent predicament of renaissance" to "a continuing renewal of adolescence in California."[41] "Unhappily," he continued, "little satisfying poetry has emerged from these births. And certainly nothing fresh. Invariably the phoenix turns out to be a throwback to the crow." On Michael Grieg's feature in *Mademoiselle,* which was the source of so much contention, and on Gilbert Sorrentino's plan for a special San Francisco issue of *Neon,* the Brooklyn journal then edited by the novelist (now at Stanford), Stock commented, "Slowly the fads filter out from New York." Although he commended Ferlinghetti's Pocket Poet Series, which specialized in "organic form," he found, "incompetence is a prime virtue in San Francisco."

Stock singled out Daniel Langton, who would subsequently contribute to *Beatitude,* for praise as a promising poet but dismissed *Inferno* editor Leslie Woolf Hedley's work as "journalese." Stock focused, however, on Kenneth Rexroth, who he believed had provided young poets "with slogans, rhetoric, attitudes and even themes," although "their stature remains in some degree the measure of his" and his "art sometimes betrays both itself and the poet's problem." Stock parodied Rexroth's autobiographical poems and mentioned as those under his influence James Harmon, Snyder, Whalen, Ron Loewinsohn, and McClure in certain of his aspects. He found Ferlinghetti more interesting in *Pictures from a Gone World* than the forthcoming *A Coney Island of the Mind,* but he attributed Ferlinghetti's success to his inimitable delivery at the poetry readings with jazz accompaniment that he had organized with Rexroth at the Cellar, a San Francisco nightclub.

When he turned to the beats, Stock became virulent in his condemnation. He believed that Ginsberg and Corso were "two poets passing through left scars." First minimizing Ginsberg as one whose "bewilderment" is possibly due to the influence of Kenneth Patchen, he went on to judge Jean McLean's "Robespierre" (a work that I have not found mentioned anywhere else) as an "excess of vituperation" against Ginsberg written in what McLean "believes to be the form of *Howl.*" Stock thought this satire of Ginsberg was not up to the original, though he found McLean's conception "less simple-minded"; he allowed that McLean might do better in the future. Stock found Ginsberg's work to be "a monument of bad, inexact taste," though it did possess "a drive that rampages through everything a poem tries to avoid," leaving one finally only with "an overwhelming sense of waste, the waste of words, the waste of the poet's spirit, and finally, the reader's waste of time."

Stock dismissed Corso much more curtly with the comment that he left "just a teeny scar" that had already vanished. "Showmanship, not poetry, is his forte," Stock asserted, recalling even the kindly Thomas Parkinson's comment that Corso was "the only untutored writer of the lot," and that his "stock in trade is impertinence" (280).

Stock observed that, when Ginsberg and Corso had left the previous winter, they claimed to be taking the renaissance with them. He believed that Daniel Langton, one of "the two or three promising young poets of the area," summed up the situation soundly when he said, "The renaissance is over, let the enlightenment begin." But Stock struck his final blow by concluding his cynical review with a sentiment that others probably shared: "One will doubt if there ever was a Renaissance."

Howl on Trial

The poetry renaissance (though Stock probably referred to the whole scene in San Francisco) thus seemed early in 1957 about to fade into a history that would question its very existence. The fauves had been in a somewhat analogous situation fifty years earlier in 1907, when their loose association was just beginning to be publicized. Painting in France at that time, however, was a dynamic, evolving art, and the advances that the fauves had made were being absorbed into new movements. The beats faced no such prospects a half-century later because the academic American poets still controlled the market, unlike the French academicians after the turn of the century.

Suddenly, however, what had appeared to be disastrous for the beats' aspirations was transformed into a windfall. The U.S. attorney had refused to institute condemnation proceedings against the City Lights Pocket Poets series edition of *Howl and Other Poems* at the behest of the collector of customs, and Capt. William Hanrahan of the juvenile department of the San Francisco police took over the crusade against what he deemed a threat to civic virtue.

Captain Hanrahan was one of those dedicated watchdogs of citizens' morals from the same kind of rigorously traditional Roman Catholic background as the city's 1970s councillor Dan White (who ended up murdering liberal major George Moscone and gay councillor Harvey Milk). He had a little list of items to be extirpated (probably not his word) from the community to make it safe for the innocent, including a list of books unfit for children to read (had it occurred to children to read them). Topping the list was *Howl*—scarcely pitched at the juvenile market. If Hanrahan could succeed in suppressing it, he planned to proceed against others.

Lawrence Ferlinghetti and Shigeyoshi Murao, who worked at the City Lights Bookshop, were booked on 1 June 1957 for publishing and selling obscene literature; the specifications originally included besides *Howl* an issue of William Margolis's magazine *The Miscellaneous Man,* but it was dropped early on. Their troubles had begun, moreover, more than two months earlier when on 25 March, collector of customs Chester MacPhee stopped part of a second shipment of *Howl* being delivered from London. He confiscated 520 copies, declaring, "The words and sense of the writing is obscene. You wouldn't want your children to come across it."[42]

On 3 April the American Civil Liberties Union informed MacPhee that it would contest the seizure. In the meantime Ferlinghetti had arranged for a third printing of the pamphlet in the United States, where it would not be under the jurisdiction of the Customs Office. On 29 May the Customs Office released the books when the federal attorney's office refused to institute condemnation proceedings.

At this point Captain Hanrahan stepped in and arrested Ferlinghetti and Murao for selling an intentionally lewd book. The ACLU posted bail, and at a trial that lasted all summer nine expert witnesses testified on the poem. Clearly the most influential of these in shaping the final decision was Berkeley professor Mark Schorer, who made a statement on the theme and structure of the poem that Judge Clayton Horn of the municipal court particularly drew upon in his decision. (Kenneth Rexroth, despite his falling out with the beats, was well disposed enough to describe *Howl* as "probably the most remarkable single poem published by a young man since the second war.")[43]

The prosecution could summon only two expert witnesses: a private elocution teacher, and David Kirk, an assistant professor of English at the Catholic University of San Francisco, who testified that "the literary value of this poem is negligible. . . . The poem is apparently dedicated to a long-dead movement, Dadaism. . . . And, therefore, the opportunity is long past for any significant literary contribution of this poem."

In his decision of 3 October 1957, Judge Horn agreed with ACLU counsel Albert Bendich's summation that the poem "does have some redeeming social importance, and . . . is not obscene." He then proceeded to deliver an explication of *Howl* based on Mark Schorer's testimony that remains one of the clearest and most succinct interpretations of not just the poem but the beat spirit behind it:

The first part of *Howl* presents a picture of a nightmare world; the second part is an indictment of those elements in modern society destructive of the best qualities of human nature; such elements are predominantly identified as materialism, conformity, and mechanization leading toward war. The third part presents a picture of an individual who is a specific representation of what the author conceives as a general condition.

"Footnote to Howl" seems to be a declamation that everything in the world is holy, including parts of the body by name. It ends in a plea for holy living.

The *San Francisco Chronicle* editorially hailed this widely applauded decision as a "landmark of law," and Judge Horn was later reelected to office. The outcome of the trial apparently discouraged Captain Hanrahan from going ahead with others, although some troubles with censorship still lay ahead for some poets with beat affinities.

It is impossible to speculate on what might have happened to the poetry renaissance if its promoters had not had this litigation forced upon them. Ferlinghetti "recommended a medal be made for Collector MacPhee, since his action was already rendering the book famous. But the police were soon to take over this advertising account and do a much better job—10,000 copies of *Howl* were in print by the time they finished with it."

It is hard to believe that a poem that so powerfully expressed the feelings of the sensitive and disturbed members of a generation would not gradually have established itself as a landmark of literature, as *Leaves of Grass* and *The Waste Land* had; but it would have been a long, painful struggle in a nation that, as Philip Whalen commented in 1971, does not have "a literate public."[44] Whitman struggled all his life for recognition that did not come until well into the next century, and Eliot's work is still condemned as purposely obscure and pedantic.

It is impossible, however, even to estimate how much Judge Horn's decision may have influenced national attention to the beats and their reception because just a month before his decision was handed down, another event occurred on the other side of the continent that far overshadowed, in its impact and the publicity it generated, his landmark decision. The beats—who had been described only four months previously in *New World Writing* as having "largely local reputations" in the Bay Area—would become international celebrities.

During the months of the trial, other poetic innovators had begun to recognize the beats. Ginsberg had been appointed a contributing editor to the Autumn 1957 issue of the *Black Mountain Review,* the house organ of a much admired experimental arts college in North Carolina where, under the leadership of Charles Olson, one of the most important groups of innovative poets in the country had gathered. The issue carried a heavy representation of the beats: selections from Kerouac's "October in the Railroad Earth," poems by Philip Whalen, Michael McClure, and Gary Snyder, and a selection from *Naked Lunch* by old sidekick William Burroughs, who was still publishing under the pseudonym William Lee. Unfortunately, this last issue of the review appeared under outside auspices because the college had been forced to close, owing to financial difficulties. (Ironically, the property was purchased as a summer retreat by Stetson University, a Southern Baptist institution.)

Olson, the former rector, moved back to Massachusetts to continue working, until his death in 1970, on his *Maximus Poems,* and his second-in-command Robert Creeley, who was already winning substantial recognition as a poet, and some of his·former students moved to the Bay Area. There they became close and valued friends of the beats and helped reinforce their position as increasingly serious and respected artists.

It is somewhat surprising, therefore, that only a year later, on 30 June 1958, Gregory Corso wrote back from Paris to Gary Snyder:

Allen and me were interviewed by syndicated funny man for masses newspaper, silly jerky and drunk interview, guy named Art Buchwald who came on sympatico, but his article sounds as if he interviewed two nowhere Bohemian cats. . . . This "beat generation" nonsense lessens the poetic intent, no wonder the academy poets keep aloft, poetry is not for public humor make-fun-of-kicks, ridiculous, the whole thing, sardine salesmen. . . .

I think mainly the reason for my silliness and Allen's in interview was because some girl from Frisco came to Paris and showed us articles and clippings of the SF scene that came on so nowhere and gloomy and bullshit and sad, that I felt inclined only to be silly.[45]

Speaking of the same period, Ginsberg complained in 1974, "The media began coming around really heavily, exploring what we were having to say and distorting it and projecting a Frankenstein vision of it all over America. . . . I realized that if our private fancies, our private poetries, were so serious that they absorbed the attention of the big, serious military generals who write for *Time* magazine, there must be something strange going on . . . the exploitation of the Beats."[46]

What had happened?

Chapter Two
Beatniks and *Beatitude*

After six years of underground circulation, Jack Kerouac's novel *On the Road* burst onto on the American scene on 5 September 1957—just after Labor Day weekend, when its potential audience was reluctantly returning from vacation or getting ready to go to college.

As Tom Clark wrote, "The confusion, excitement, drinking, and total disordering of Kerouac's private life that accompanied the publication of *On the Road* was no dream."[1] This pathetic story has already been told in detail by Kerouac's biographers, and his downfall has been amply hooted by his detractors. There is no need to linger over it here; Kerouac's history would actually have only a tangential connection to the San Francisco Poetry Renaissance. Kerouac spent relatively little time in the Bay Area after becoming a celebrity. Just before the publication of *On the Road,* he had made an attempt to move his mother to Berkeley in May 1957 and to settle there. But this experiment lasted only six weeks, and before the novel appeared they were in Orlando, Florida. Mother Gabrielle, as Clark reported, "was ill-disposed toward Berkeley from the start; she hated the fog, feared earthquakes, [and] felt 'lonely and idle' "(156–57). Furthermore, the publication of the novel, rather than restoring the bond between Kerouac and Neal Cassady, led to a cooling of relations between them.

The purpose of this book, in any event, is to point out the previously underacknowledged positive accomplishments of the beat poets rather than to dwell, as so many have before, on the damage done by the beatniks. Actually, the ultimately destructive, excessive publicity in national magazines did not develop until 1959, after what the forces of respectability thought the damage done by *On the Road* had been compounded in 1958 by *The Dharma Bums,* which much more radically challenged the prevailing American lifestyle than its downbeat and almost universally misread predecessor.[2] The "Frankenstein vision" that Ginsberg protested earlier was principally found in the ephemeral writings of local newspapers; these reviews might soon have been forgotten if the Luce empire newsmagazines had not seized on the beats as a possible source of some provocative features in the last dreary days of the Eisenhower administration.

The first agitated reactions had come from those who had the most to gain or lose by the success of the beats—those who sought to shape and control the tastes of the nation's small but influential audience for serious literature. After arguing in *New World Writing* that "there is no question but that the San Francisco renaissance is radically different from what is going on elsewhere," Kenneth Rexroth went on to protest bitterly that there was only one trouble with this renaissance: "It is too far away from the literary market place. . . . Distance from New York City [makes] it harder to get things, if not published, at least nationally circulated."[3] It was not too far away, however, to catch the roving eye of Barney Rosset, a shrewd, daring, and dedicated enterpreneur. His Grove Press was posing a serious challenge to New York's aging, genteel publishing houses in an effort to win the audience of young readers who were becoming increasingly disaffected by the effete academicism of the most heavily promoted new fiction and poetry.

After *New World Writing* published Rexroth's essay, it avoided the beats before it expired with its June 1959 issue; the editors thought it was time to "pass their mantles along," since "what was considered *avant garde* in 1951 . . . is likely to be far more widely read today."[4] Among *New World Writing*'s heirs were the *Chicago Review* and the *Hudson Review,* of which we shall hear more shortly. Although it had seemed like a breath of fresh air through long-unopened windows in its early days, *New World Writing* now seems to have been—as it had to be to survive in an age of paranoia—quite cautious and principally devoted to developing an American audience for international literature. Its publishers probably found the challenges of the 1960s more than they wished to take on. Barney Rosset was waiting to take over the job.

A Friend Afar: *Evergreen Review*

Rosset had launched Grove Press back in 1949 as a modest venture of a kind common in Greenwich Village, though the aim of the at first exclusively paperback operation was not to produce another little magazine or series of chapbooks but to bring back into print what the proprietor regarded as important works long unavailable in the United States. His first offering was a most appropriate one for a publisher who would later become allied with the beats: the first reprinting—nearly a century after its publication and quick disappearance—of the last novel that Herman Melville published during his lifetime, *The Confidence Man* (1857). This novel was a cryptic, downbeat, picaresque account of the activities of a chameleonlike "cosmopolitan" on a road resembling Kerouac's, this road being provided by the Mississippi River and its racing steamboats.

Most of Rosset's next choices for reprint were titles that would have won the approval of the editors of *New World Writing*—Richard Crashaw's English verse, Henry James's *The Sacred Fount,* Philip Spencer's biography of Flaubert, Donald Keene's introduction to Japanese literature, Samuel Beckett's *Molloy.* But a hint of what was to come was provided quite early by his publication of an eyebrow-raising selection (by Simone de Beauvoir) of the works of the Marquis de Sade. Most of Rosset's titles, however, were aimed at a discriminating audience. He finally scored the coup he must have been hoping for with the first American edition of a work that became an enormous cult favorite, Samuel Beckett's nihilist play that exactly mirrored the mood of American intellectuals in the 1950s, *Waiting for Godot.* He followed up with a reprinting of Robert Lindner's 1944 *Rebel without a Cause.* Heartened by his successes (including Jean Genet's *The Maids*), Rosset then decided to launch as the fifty-ninth title in his Evergreen Books Series a quarterly review early in 1957.

The first issue of *Evergreen Review* was tastefully printed with large type, featured a portfolio of photographs of touching vignettes of American life by Harold Feinstein, and was simply a miscellany with no visible theme; unlike other such ventures, it even lacked an introductory editorial providing a rationale for the undertaking. It included an interview with Jean-Paul Sartre in which he explained his break with the Communist party after Russia's suppression of the 1956 Hungarian rebellion; prose and poetry by Samuel Beckett; one of the first appearances in an American publication of a James Purdy short story; and a transcription of jazz drummer Baby Dodds's account of his life. Buried near the back of the issue, and deemphasized on the back-cover blurbs, was what was surely its raison d'être—an essay by University of California English professor Mark Schorer (who was then at work on the mammoth biography of Sinclair Lewis that he was to grow to hate but that became the model for such projects). "On *Lady Chatterley's Lover*" concluded with Schorer's impassioned statement, "The pathos of Lawrence's novel arises from the tragedy of modern society. What is tragic is that we cannot feel our tragedy."[5] There is no clue anywhere in the issue that Barney Rosset would publish, as he must already have been planning, the first above-the-counter version of D. H. Lawrence's titillating novel in the United States and would challenge existing censorship practices until he and the novel were vindicated. Nor could anyone have suspected then that Mark Schorer would be the heroic voice behind the proceedings to be reported less than a year later in the fourth issue of *Evergreen Review.*

With its second issue, however, *Evergreen Review* found a direction and a purpose. The entire issue was devoted to the "San Francisco Scene." There is no internal indication when the contents were selected, but it must have been before the *Howl* trial began for there was no mention of the U.S. customs and police actions against *Howl,* which appeared without its "Footnote" at the end of the issue. (One line was expurgated and appeared as, "who let themselves be . . . . . . in the . . . by saintly motorcyclists, and screamed with joy"—as it also appears in the original City Lights edition.)

The issue led off with a "San Francisco Letter" from Kenneth Rexroth that made clear his impatience with local publicity even before the *Howl* trial. This was followed by one of his poems, selections from Brother Antoninus (William Everson), Robert Duncan, Lawrence Ferlinghetti, Henry Miller (praising "Big Sur and the Good Life"), Michael McClure, Josephine Miles, Jack Spicer, Michael Rumaker, filmmaker James Broughton, Gary Snyder ("The Berry Feast"), Philip Whalen, Jack Kerouac, *Howl,* Ralph J. Gleason on the city's jazz scene, Dore Ashton on the city's school of painters, and photographs by Henry Redl of eight poets.

Kenneth Rexroth's letter got the unprecedented collage off to a downbeat start: "There has been so much publicity recently about the San Francisco Renaissance and the New Generation of Revolt and Our Underground Literature and Cultural Disaffiliation that I for one am getting a little sick of writing about it, and the writers who are the objects of all the uproar run the serious danger of falling over 'dizzy with success' in the immortal words of Comrade Koba [whoever that may be]." By the time the man who might have laid claim to discovering the beats dispatched this message, all was not well between him and them, although from New York he probably still seemed to be the authority on the distant scene. After giving New York and "fake" New Orleans their licks, Rexroth announced that San Francisco was the only place he could live in the United States: "I always feel like I ought to get a passport every time I cross the Bay to Oakland or Berkeley." He went on to inform the unenlightened that "no literature of the past two hundred years is of the slightest importance unless it is 'disaffiliated,' " ranted at some length against materialistic capitalism, then finally discussed individuals. He provided capsule biographies of William Everson, Philip Lamantia, Robert Duncan, Allen Ginsberg, and Lawrence Ferlinghetti, stressing particularly the poetry/jazz readings they were presenting at the Cellar. Rexroth concluded with the comment that Everson, Duncan, Ferlinghetti, and Ginsberg were saying exactly the same thing—"I suppose, in a religious age, it would be called religious poetry, all of it. Today we have to call it anarchism. A fellow over in Africa [Albert Schweitzer?] calls it 'reverence for life.' "[6] He simply ignored Kerouac, Whalen, and Snyder, among others.

Following this issue, *Evergreen Review* did not become strictly an outlet for the beats, though it did continue to give them sympathetic representation, despite an acerbic quarrel with Jack Kerouac, whose contribution to the "San Francisco Scene" was supposed to have been a cut version of his novel *The Subterraneans*. When he saw the proofs, he called the "60 percent cut" a "castration" and insisted that his work had to be published "as it is or not at all." Old reliable "October in the Railroad Earth" was substituted, but Grove did go ahead and publish the novel "restored to its original state."[7]

The third issue returned to the miscellany format, this time internationally flavored by contributions from Beckett, Ionesco, and Robbe-Grillet along with works of Frank O'Hara and William Carlos Williams, a kind of father figure to the beats. There were also three poems by Gregory Corso, omitted from the previous issue, and a letter from Gary Snyder in Kyoto. The beats once more dominated the fourth issue, perhaps unintentionally. It included Lawrence Ferlinghetti's "Horn on *Howl*," the report of the San Francisco obscenity trial, which seems to have been rushed into print at the last moment; it appeared in the back of the magazine and was not emphasized on the cover blurbs. The issue also contained Ginsberg's eighteen-page poem "Siesta in Xbalba and Return to the States," which depicted his "—Returning / armed with New Testament" from the ancient ruined cities of Mexico to "The nation over the border [that] / grinds its arms and dreams / of war."[8] Jack Kerouac's "Seattle Burlesque" and a poem by Robin Blaser (a friend of Robert Duncan's who by then had gone to Boston), rounded out the beat contribution to the fourth issue.

Foes Afield: The New York Establishment

The beats maintained a presence in the quarterly through 1958, though they were subordinated to Rosset's new interests; for instance, the seventh issue was entirely devoted to new Mexican writing. Meanwhile, the New York publications were not taking well to the beats. The denunciations came, as might be expected, from those who had the most to lose by the possible ascendancy of the wild beasts from the West—the decorous academic poets writing the elegant reviews that were their publishing homes. The most famous of these putdowns—by Norman Podhoretz in *Partisan Review* and by John Ciardi in the *Saturday Review*—have often been reprinted as token voices of the opposition, but the most venomous attacks were launched earlier, in the Autumn 1957 issue of the *Hudson Review*. Because they appeared in this inconspicuous context they have escaped attention.

The *Hudson Review* was founded immediately after World War II to try to counter the distressing image of New York as a center of proletarian radicalism and to reestablish the kind of Henry Jamesean salon society that its editors fantasized had once existed in Gotham. It was designed to avoid all possibly embarrassing philosophical or political commitments and to devote itself to nothing but the advancement of the interests of its band of regular contributors. The beats, motivated by an ideal of spiritual regeneration through a literary medium, had to be put down as hopelessly vulgar if the *Hudson Review*'s chosen were to hold the ground they were winning in American literature anthologies.

In the Autumn 1957 issue, Louis Simpson, a Ph.D. candidate at Columbia en route to Berkeley, tacked to the end of his review about the lack of any responsible criticism of poetry in the United States, "Poets in Isolation," a comment dripping with the section-man sarcasm that J. D. Salinger had castigated in "Franny": "I wish to add my voice to the chorus of praise of the new Californian school of poets, located in Los Angeles. I am astonished that William Carlos Williams, *Mademoiselle* magazine, and Mr. [Harvey] Breit of the *New York Times* [all of whom had shown a favorable interest in the beats] have not yet discovered this youthful group of young poets (not one of them a day over thirty-five). It is true they have not written much poetry as yet, and most of what they have written is unreadable." (Simpson was thirty-four at the time.) He then reproduced lines from their "solitary, supreme masterpiece, 'Squeal,' " borrowing Ginsberg's opening charge in *Howl:*

> I saw the best minds of my generation
> Destroyed. . . .
> They came from all over, from the pool-room,
> The bargain basement, the rod,
> From Whitman, from Parkersburg, Rimbaud. . . .
> Reading their poems to Vassar girls,
> Being interviewed by *Mademoiselle.* . . .[9]

Earlier in the same issue, Simpson, who seemed particularly upset by the beats' recognition by the well-paying *Mademoiselle* (which, like some other fashion magazines, was trying to enhance its image as a patron of high culture by soliciting contributions from respected writers like Tennessee

Williams), offered one of his own poems. It was representative of the work of the many "me, too" aspirants of that era in its demonstration that T. S. Eliot's *Waste Land* tradition must be kept alive by rehashing it:

> This is the New England, rocks and brush
> Where none may live but only tigers, parrots
> And mute imagining . . .
> America, a desert with a name.[10]

In the next issue of *Hudson Review*, fashionable critic Benjamin DeMott took a brief disdainful look at the recently published *On the Road* in a review of several new novels: "Consider for example the second novel of Mr. Jack Kerouac, late of the football team at Columbia. The book's claims have to be acknowledged: one of the Quality Magazines speaks of it as a work of great vigor and drive and considering its author's relations with the West Coast howlers, to ignore it would be to ignore a New School." He found, however, that "this kind of writing makes its reader feel badly . . . like a slob running a temperature of 103.6."[11]

Because Simpson's and DeMott's spleen was buried in obscure reviews, no interested parties appear to have spotted them at the time—except for an offended group of poets in Los Angeles of whose existence Simpson was apparently entirely unaware when he contrived his parody. In an editorial in *Coastlines*, "A Squawk about 'Squeal,' " Gene Frumkin, representing a group that was already annoyed with the beats, asked about Simpson, "What if he has confused us with a bunch up in San Francisco? After all, down here we are so unknown that we have barely heard of ourselves. . . . Anyway, it must be dreadful to think the only readers of one's poems are professors and editors and fellow poets who immediately begin dismembering them, probably through habit, instead of keeping the poems whole long enough to feel them."[12]

No such problems of obscurity kept Norman Podhoretz's distaste under wraps. He had his first brief go at the beats in the *New Republic* in September 1957, but that was only a warm-up for his big challenge in the Spring 1958 issue of *Partisan Review* (which had begun as a fiery supporter of the Communist party in the 1930s but broke with it after the Stalinist purges and became a forum for the discussion of the great besetting problems of the time). Podhoretz's diatribe has been frequently reprinted as the prototypical genteel assault upon the beats. He began with a portrayal of Jack Kerouac as "the spokesman of a new group of rebels and Bohemians" whose "photogenic countenance (unshaven, of course, and topped by an unruly crop of black hair falling over his forehead) was showing up in various mass-circulation magazines" (305).[13] This characterization led Podhoretz to his apparently principal point that a "tremendous emphasis on emotional intensity, this notion that to be hopped-up is the most desirable of all human conditions, lies at the heart of the Beat Generation ethos and distinguishes it radically from the Bohemianism of the past" (307). Podhoretz seemed to to be trying to present himself as dispassionate, well-mannered, and urbane. But after fidgeting through passages of doth-protest-too-much homophobia and pure jealousy of lively writing styles, one finds that he was really motivated by a neurotic terror: he asserted that "the plain truth is that the primitivism of the Beat Generation serves first of all as a cover for an anti-intellectualism so bitter that it makes the ordinary American's hatred of eggheads seem positively benign" (313). This observation led to the surprising charge that the beats' "worship of primitivism and spontaneity . . . arises from a pathetic poverty of feeling as well" (315). "To tell the truth," Podhoretz confessed, "whenever I hear anyone talking about instinct and being and the secrets of human energy, I get nervous; next thing you know he'll be saying violence is just fine" (316). He heard in "even the relatively mild ethos of Kerouac's books . . . a suppressed cry: Kill the intellectuals who can talk coherently, kill the people who can sit still for five minutes at a time, kill those incomprehensible characters who are capable of getting seriously involved with a woman, a job, a cause" (318). This was a strange response to works like *Howl,* which ends, "Holy the supernatural extra brilliant intelligent kindness of the soul," and to a philosophy that stressed "*unworldly love* that has *no hope* of the world and cannot change the world to its desire."

Leroi Jones in his beat days appeared to be exactly on target when he observed:

It would seem that Norman Podhoretz in his article "The Know-Nothing Beats" objected more violently to certain instances of socio-ethical non-conformity in the Beat Generation than to its paucity of erudition, as the title of his essay states. . . . I have read a great many of these scathing rants that are being palmed off as objective critical studies of the "New Bohemianism," and always without exception they have come down from the small coteries of quasi-novelists or *New Yorker* suburban intellectual types of the late '40's and early '50's which represents [*sic*] so much of what Beat is a reaction against . . . as it is also against what Randall Jarrell calls "The Age of Criticism."[14]

This is from the beginning of a letter that Jones wrote to the *Partisan Review,* for which his wife Hettie was advertising and business manager. Excerpts from the letter appeared in a subsequent issue of the review, although it has been difficult to locate because correspondence of this kind was not included in a comprehensive index to the magazine that appeared in 1966. While it is difficult to evaluate Jone's letter as a whole from fragments attacking parts of Podhoretz's arguments, his initial criticism uncovered the true nature of critically "objective" attacks: they were the frightened cries of those who feared for the personal security they had schemed so hard to win.

Such fears certainly also inspired another contribution to *Partisan Review* a year after Podhoretz's; Diana Trilling was a card-carrying member of the older generation of the Columbia University literary establishment, but her essay "The Other Night at Columbia" was a genuinely urbane and—as she could afford to make it—far more generous and understanding if still wrist-slapping verdict on the beats than Podhoretz's had been. She described a "Beat" reading by Ginsberg, Gregory Corso, and Peter Orlovsky before a student group at Columbia that she attended with some other faculty wives. She has been pilloried particularly for her reminiscences in this account of how Ginsberg had given evidence of "his present talent for self-promotion" back in his student days, when she had found him "a troublesome young man, who had managed to break through the barrier of student anonymity" by pestering her distinguished husband Lionel. In her essay she defended "the expectation that a student at Columbia would do his work, submit it to his teachers through the normal channels of communication, stay out of jail," and wait to see what success, if any, he enjoyed.[15]

She became the laughingstock of a group whose opinion she probably did not much value anyway when Robert Bly published in his occasional magazine, *The Fifties,* "The Other Night in Heaven," attributed to a Diana Tilling. Beginning with the statement that "I am very important," as was also her husband Lionel, this account of attending a Ginsberg reading ended up:

When I got home, I found in our comfortably-furnished living room a comfortable professional meeting going on. I found there Pope John, Charlie Chaplin, Boris Pasternak, Daddy Warbucks, William Phillips, Randall Jarrell, Smiling Jack, W. H. Auden, Henry Ford, Picasso, The Dean of Canterbury, Mao Tse Tung, the Wright Brothers, The Hathaway Man, Jacques Barzun, Stephen Markmus, Robert Hall, and Henry Luce. To find your living-room so full is the reward of being a successful writer in America.[16]

This droll parody, bringing together international political and religious leaders and comic-strip characters, nevertheless missed the point of the original article: Diana Trilling was not a celebrity headhunter; like most upper–middle class New York women—especially those of Jewish descent who had, as she stressed herself, suffered the hurt of anti-Semitism in the 1930s—she wanted to protect and share (like the beats) with a small circle of friends their hard-won comfort and security. In her article, she spoke of being "moved" by Ginsberg's reading, but she felt put in her place by W. H. Auden's stricture that she should not have been. (Auden and Barzun were indeed waiting in her living room after the reading; she probably would not have been comfortable with all the other unlikely guests Robert Bly assembled.) What concerned Trilling was that people should proceed through "normal channels of communication," as she and her husband had had to do and still did. Breaking barriers was a dangerous business.

Bly's failure to hit this particular target was not surprising, however, since he was himself a celebrity headhunter and a more captivating performer than the beats were. He actually showed little interest in them, and he was more likely burlesquing Diana Trilling for her treatment of poets without New York credentials than for her comments on the beats specifically. The only comment that he made about the beats in his irregularly issued magazine (*The Fifties* became *The Sixties,* and then *The Seventies,* over only nine numbers) occurred in a 1959 article on Robert Creeley: his poems "and those of the entire Black Mountain and San Francisco groups, are based entirely, it seems to me, on an American tradition [that] is not rich enough; it is short, Puritanical, and has only one or two first-rate poets in it." He feared "they will go the way of Sandburg" and the Chicago group of the 1910s; "in both movements there is the thought that poetry can only be written by the uncorrupted and innocent."[17] He devoted most of his magazine to translations (some his own) of European poets he thought too little known in the United States. In 1962 he did use his nom de plume, "Crunk," for an essay on Gary Snyder's poetry, which he found "very different" from that of beat poets, displaying "a certain gentleness and care for civilization . . . utterly absent in Ginsberg and Orlovsky," whom he joined Podhoretz in unwarrantedly branding as "opposed to civilization of all kinds."[18]

The angriest and most persistent vendetta against the beats came from the most influential critic—who had the most to lose should they have a substantial impact on national taste—and did not begin until 1959, culminating in 1960 as the poetry renaissance was ending. John Ciardi, although not held in the highest esteem by most of his academic contemporaries, reveled in styling himself America's first poet-millionaire as a result of the extraordinary response to his imaginative translation of Dante's *Divine Comedy,* which won new audiences for the classic. From the conspicuous eminence of his weekly columns for Norman Cousins's intellectual bargain basement, the *Saturday Review* (no longer by 1960 . . . *of Literature*), Ciardi kept poetry a livelier topic than one might have imagined possible in Eisenhower's America by attacking beloved icons like Anne Morrow Lindbergh.

In 1960 he had a go at the beats—who were already on the ropes as a result of media attention to beatnik squalor—in "Epitaph for the Dead Beats." As the title suggested, he did not bother to attack the poets as a living force but set out to provide their postmortem. He tempered his supercilious judgments with the concession that, "were it a simple choice between going Madison Avenue and going beat, I should certainly insist that the Beat has all the merit on its side," intimating inescapably that Ciardi himself provided an alternative to these extremes.[19]

Reading the essay today, it is poignantly transparent that this diatribe resulted from Ciardi's outrage that his godfather position was being challenged. He repeated the familiar cliché about anyone over thirty being considered "the enemy"—though the beats themselves "are over the line into enemy territory" (12)—as well as the one about the beats insisting upon conformity as much as those they were protesting against. Why the beats distrusted the previous generation, however, is apparent from old daddy Ciardi's version of the traditional "You don't know what hard times are, boy" line: "Had the Beats reached their early twenties in time for the Depression bread lines or the army's dreary combination of foxholes and boredom, they would certainly have found other business than the elaborate cultivation of their sensations and of their purified sacred impulses" (12).

As one reads on, it becomes embarrassingly clear that Ciardi was not at all acquainted with the beats beyond Ginsberg's poems and sensational press reports about Kerouac's fiction and his behavior. What he says does not apply to Whalen, McClure, Snyder, or poet-entrepreneur Ferlinghetti but only to what Thomas Parkinson differentiated from them as "incompetent and non-productive" beatniks. Ciardi's "epitaph" has no relevance for those to whom it allegedly applied but was obviously devised to reassure the aging readers of the *Saturday Review* who were wringing their hands wondering what the world was coming to and cheerlessly contemplating how their own epitaphs might read.

The most regrettable indication of Ciardi's refusal to acknowledge what was happening in the world that was passing him and his readers by was his sign-off: "I hope the next time the young go out for an intellectual rebellion, they will think to try the library. . . . Even rebels can find it useful to know something, if only to learn to sit still with a book in hand" (42). The productive beats were actually quite sophisticated readers. Kerouac headed for the library when he dropped out of close-order drill at Navy boot camp in protest against boring conformity, and Ginsberg's work, like Whalen's, is sometimes criticized for bristling with too many literary allusions. Whalen and Snyder were Buddhist scholars. It was the next rebellious generation, the hippies and yippies, who ignored the library; if intellectuals had made common cause with the beats, there might not have subsequently been so few of either around.

The basic tragic flaw of self-seekers like Podhoretz, Diana Trilling, and Ciardi, all of whom might have strengthened the national intellectual fiber if they had put aside their vanity and supported the beats, is most startlingly illustrated from a surprising source—an account of Allen Ginsberg's visit to India in 1962 by an American observer. In "Ginsberg among the Hindus," Michael Renner portrayed the poet's reception in Bombay, where he had come to "corroborate his own view of life with India's eternal philosophy," only to find "his hosts only possessing a vague familiarity with either. . . . Communication with Bombay's self-consciously Westernized intellectuals had not been rendered impossible by any fatal difference between the Oriental soul (which Ginsberg sought to explore) and the Occidental mind. Both used the idiom of the modern West but Ginsberg, the rebel, was fleeing the very civilization the Indians were assiduously cultivating."[20]

Renner wound up with a touching account of a Westernized Indian couple's response to Ginsberg's reading in Calcutta: the husband, a businessman aspiring to British acceptance, felt "confused, somewhat embarrassed," but sat erect and proper while his small Brahmin wife folded her knitting "and with the slightest hint of determination on her face calmly arose and walked slowly through the door."[21]

The very bourgeois materialism that Ginsberg was attacking in *Howl* for having corrupted America was poisoning those in the lands where he had hoped to find regeneration. It was unlikely that any movement of the "wild beasts" (fauve or beat) toward "unconditioned mind" could dispel the introverted greed that Veblen dubbed "conspicuous consumption" any more than William Morris's arts and crafts movement in the Victorian twilight did. Such a beat influence was especially unlikely as long as those who, like John Ciardi, believed that there was "reason enough for the young to rebel from patterns of American complacency" nevertheless became so addicted to la dolce vita that they cynically wrote premature obituaries for those advocating alternatives.[22]

Fixing Chicago's *Big Table*

What happened in Chicago when rebellious spirits tried to create an alternative provides a bitterly edifying lesson. There had always been a few artistic souls in America's "second city" striving to develop it into a midland cultural capital. But Chicago's artistic renaissance following the Great White City Exposition of 1893, which was supposed to have set the course for the coming century, had been diverted to the more inviting Atlantic and Pacific coasts, leaving only Harriet Monroe's tastemaking *Poetry* magazine on Lake Michigan's shores as a power base for the literati.

As demonstrated by Chicago's successive failures to establish itself as a jazz center, a radio capital, or a television capital, the city's problems were not external competition so much as internal ineptitude. The Midwest bastion of isolation and political reaction that took its label *Tribuneland* from Colonel Robert McCormick's pacesetting newspaper was not likely to prove a rewarding dwelling place for the muses. And although the Rockefellers' University of Chicago did become one of the most outstanding academic institutions in the country, it became almost as sheltered as a medieval monastery, existing in tense isolation from the decaying neighborhood around it.

The *Chicago Review* had been founded after World War II mainly as a graduate student project to provide the region with a parallel to New York's *Partisan* and *Hudson* reviews; but uncharacteristically for an academic journal, it had often shown a distressing interest in populist culture. Under the dynamic editorship of Irving Rosenthal, the *Chicago Review* was attracted early to the beats and featured them in all of its 1958 issues.

The Spring Issue, devoted to "Ten San Francisco Poets," opened with poems by veterans of the 1955 Six Gallery reading—Ginsberg, Whalen, Lamantia, McClure—along with Kerouac, Ferlinghetti, John Wieners, Robert Duncan, and Kirby Doyle (a friend of Lew Welch's who did not publish his first book until 1966), followed by an excerpt from Burrough's *Naked Lunch*. The forms of the poems included and the sensibilities they exhibited were more diversified than usual in beat collages; as a result, they came across as samples of the works of highly individualistic artists working in the same area, as the beats preferred, rather than as specimens of some collective vision. Kerouac's opening "The Wheel of the Quivering Meat Conception" has a characteristically downbeat ending: "I wish I was free / of that slaving meat wheel / and safe in heaven dead."[23] But it does not set the tone for the joy radiating from "madman Allen" Ginsberg's discovery in "Malest Cornifici Tuo Catullo" of the thrill of "a new young cat / and my imagination of eternity's boy" (12), nor for the withering tone of Philip

Whalen's concluding comparison in "10:X:57, Forty-five Years since the Fall of the Ch'ing Dynasty"—between Jimmy Dean being mobbed by "all these monster teen-age hoods" and "the United States Marines building teakwood campfires / Out of the Empress's bedroom furniture on the Phoenix-Viewing / Terrace toasting their wienies" (24).

This issue began with two brief statements by Ferlinghetti and Kerouac about San Francisco as the center of a poetry renaissance after the *Howl* trial. Ferlinghetti's "Note on Poetry in San Francisco" maintained that this poetry was "not a school nor does it have any definite regional characteristics." He maintained that it was "quite different from the 'poetry about poetry,' the poetry of technique, the poetry for poets and professors which has dominated the quarterlies and anthologies in this country for some time"; rather, San Francisco poets were putting "poetry back into the street where it once was." The renaissance marked "the beginning of a very inevitable thing— the *resocialization* of poetry. But not like the Thirties" (4).

Jack Kerouac's "The Origins of Joy in Poetry" saw the renaissance works as street poetry also, but he emphasized their being "a kind of new-old Zen Lunacy poetry . . . diametrically opposed to the Eliot shot" (3). Both of these commentators championed populist views of poetry; but the difference between them suggests one reason why Ferlinghetti held himself as a poet somewhat apart from the beats he sponsored. His was essentially a sociopolitical view of poetry that emphasized the words of the song, while Kerouac's introspective view focused on the singer (he admitted, for example, that "in spite of the dry rules [Eliot] set down his poetry itself is sublime"). The prevalence of Kerouac's view among other poets and young audiences is one reason the beats, like the fauves, never became an organized movement seeking to displace an Establishment and instead remained a group of outsiders transiently banded together.

The *Chicago Review,* unlike even the *Evergreen Review,* was not content with a single tribute to the San Franciscans. Its next two issues gave increasing space to the beats, with a large part of the summer issue devoted to Zen-inspired works. Bigoted Chicago became restive. When a fourth such issue (Winter 1958–59) was readied, featuring further material from William Burroughs's work in progress, the storm broke. After a bitter dialogue with jittery university officials, who were concerned about the support of conservative alumni and the always unstable relations with the community, led to the suppression of the issue, the editors, with one exception, joined to found *Big Table* as an independent journal. Its first issue consisted of the contents of the suppressed issue of *Chicago Review.* Ginsberg and Corso came to campus on 29 January 1959 for a fund-raiser to support the new journal.

Big Table was not to enjoy, however, a long or rewarding life. Under the editorship of Paul Carrol, the second issue carried excerpts from Edward Dahlberg's autobiography-in-progress *Because I Was Flesh*. (Since Dahlberg, one of the proletarian novelists of the 1930s, by this time nearly sixty and nearly forgotten, had grown up in Kansas City, Missouri, he was seized upon by the Midwesterners as their contribution to the Beat Generation.) The third issue included Allen Ginsberg's "Kaddish" and works by the controversial Norman Mailer, the disreputable hustler John Rechy, and New York's promising John Ashbery, as well as a large foldout reproduction of abstract expressionist painter Franz Kline's *Mister*. The editors announced, however, that a sixth issue would consist of a symposium on post-Christian man in which beat sympathizer Paul Goodman would be joined by distinctly non-beat thinkers such as Allen Tate, Russell Kirk, and William Phillips (sometime of the *Partisan Review*).

These plans never came to fruition, however, for in March 1959 the U.S. Post Office banned the mailing of the fifth issue and impounded 499 copies. A sequel to San Francisco's *Howl* trial ensued, in which distinguished literary figures such as Jacques Barzun, Lionel Trilling, and John Ciardi surprisingly joined Ferlinghetti, Ginsberg, Norman Mailer, Pierre DeLattre, and others in defense of the magazine. The best expert witness the government could recruit this time was Wisconsin's August Derleth, writer of local color and horror stories (and proprietor of Arkham House, which was principally devoted to keeping alive the memory of Rhode Island's master of the weird tale, H. P. Lovecraft). On 5 July 1960 Judge Julius J. Hoffman set aside the ban on the magazine, but by that time cult enthusiasm for *Big Table* and the beats had run its course.

While legal problems kept *Big Table* under wraps through most of 1959, the image of the degenerate beatniks fabricated by the mass media thwarted literary journals' attempts to call attention to the beats' creative efforts to shock American society into recognizing its shortcomings.

Life among the Beatniks

Probably the most conspicuous and most disastrous publicity that the beats received was from two features in Henry Luce's *Life*, neither of which had much to do with the poetry renaissance.

The first appeared in the 21 September 1959 issue just as schools and colleges were opening for the new season. It established the terms in which the increasingly contentious discussion would be conducted with its title, "Squaresville U.S.A. vs. Beatsville." What may puzzle later readers is that the article was based not on the beat enclave in San Francisco's North Beach but on the decaying Los Angeles seaside suburb called Venice West (to be discussed in Chapter 5). Suffice to say that Venice West was the preserve of Lawrence Lipton, whose *The Holy Barbarians* (1959) claimed to be "the first complete inside story of the Beat Generation," although it was principally about beatniks.

According to *Life,* three silly high school girls in Hutchinson, Kansas, bored with life at "the world's salt capital," one hot summer's day had impulsively invited Lipton to visit town for a "cool-in." When Lipton, never one to turn down a chance to peddle his wares for a bit of bread, accepted, the girls were nonplussed and decided that they had better disinvite him. This action was strongly supported by the community as well as by the local gendarmerie, which passed the authoritative word that "a beatnik doesn't like to work, any man who doesn't like to work is a vagrant, and a vagrant goes to jail around here."[24] The editors of *Life,* desperate for some provocative copy during the summer dog days, made a seven-page feature out of this microcosmic confrontation between Main Street U.S.A. and the new breed of medicine men. Using some of the tackiest photographs of the decade, they matched scenes from the good life in western Kansas with pictures of the degenerate beatnik haunts in what looks like a still very crew-cut Venice, California.

The story elicited the hoped-for outraged responses. *Life's* letters section for 12 October included defenses not only of the attractions of Hutchinson but of the charms of Venice ("real canals") outside the beat colony, which longtime residents had not welcomed. Bruce E. Hunsberger from Reading, Pennsylvania ("the world's pretzel capital"), pronounced that "Beat is conformity to the greatest degree; it is conformity to God and nature and man in one force working together."[25]

Paul O'Neil was not ready to go along with this lofty sentiment in "The Only Rebellion Around," the most substantial rumination on the beats to appear in a mass-circulation magazine (*Life*) and the one that would be most frequently quoted and reprinted. O'Neil's ambiguous and indecisive account does demonstrate the extent, however, to which the beats had begun to challenge complacent American thinking as the Eisenhower fifties dragged to their dreary end. His appearance in *Life* also illustrates the Luce empire's uncertainty about which bandwagon it should board to keep circulation healthy.

Although overstated for the benefit of an audience that could not take in the implications of new ideas quickly, O'Neil began with an explanation that is accurate from a materialistic point of view:

Beat philosophy seems calculated to offend the whole population, civil, military and ecclesiastic—particularly and ironically those radicals of only yesterday who demanded a better world for the ill-fed, ill-clothed and ill-housed of the Great Depression and who still breathe heavily from proclaiming man's right to work and organize. Hard-core Beats want freedom to disorganize and thus to ensure full flowering of their remarkable individualities. . . . The Beat Generation can be much more accurately described as a cult of the Pariah. It yearns for the roach-guarded mores of the skid road, the flophouse, the hobo jungle and the slum, primarily to escape regimentation.[26]

"Not like the Thirties," Ferlinghetti had emphasized, but O'Neil would have found it difficult to impose the image he manufactured on an imaginative and successful entrepreneur like Ferlinghetti. He was obliged to admit that the Beat Generation "has attracted wide public attention and is exerting astonishing influence" (116), citing the appearance of some of its adherents in radio soap operas and national comic strips. Rejecting arguments that the beat cult really began to form in 1947 (as it did, with the travels of Kerouac and Neal Cassady), O'Neil wrongly dated it from 1953 (when nothing relevant happened). He described the beat poets as "dissidents so enthralled with their own egos and so intent on bitter personal complaint that they would be incapable of organizing juvenile delinquents in a reform school" (119). (Nearly all attacks on the beats were based on this period's pervasive tenet that everything had to be as "organized," as Caribbean cruises for bored retirees or the guidebooks that the Luce publications churned out to try to prescribe a uniform national viewpoint on everything from cuisine to history.) "The bulk of the Beat writers," O'Neil raged on, "are undisciplined and slovenly amateurs who have deluded themselves into believing their lugubrious absurdities are art simply because they have rejected the form, style and attitudes of previous generations and have seized upon obscenity as an expression of 'total personality' " (125). Yet, in a sudden reversal, he attacked those critics who "discount all Beat literature," for "a few Beat writers demonstrate that gift of phrase and those flashes of insight which bespeak genuine talent" (126). He concluded: "The Beat Generation is not alone in the U.S. in questioning the values of contemporary society, in feeling spiritually stifled by present-day materialism, and in growing restive at the conformity which seems to be the price of security. But only the Beats have actually been moved to reject contemporary society in voicing their quarrel with these values. . . . A hundred million squares must ask themselves: 'What have we done to deserve this?' " (130).

If this poignant question was ever answered, it was not in *Life*. After

O'Neil's article, the magazine mentioned the beats only once again (2 April 1960) in a brief notice of two beat candidates who were running in an election in Fort Worth, Texas, but even the outcome of these contests went unreported.

For a more graphic picture of beat life, one could go to the movies. The term "Beat Generation" had gained sufficient currency by 1959 to serve as the title of one of the dying breed of "B" pictures—low-budget films produced quickly and usually thoughtlessly since the depression years when they filled out double features at neighborhood theaters and drive-ins. Albert Zugsmith's opus for Hollywood's ailing giant, Metro-Goldwyn-Mayer, introduced Squaresville to the lifestyle deplored in O'Neil's article. Actually, Zugsmith sought to sound a much stronger warning against the beat peril than *Life* had: *The Beat Generation* unwound the lurid story of a psychopathic culprit (played by Ray Danton) who when not assaulting housewives wallowed in drink at a beatnik bar. *New York Times* reviewer Howard Thompson warned that "*The Beat Generation* is enough to make any member or non-member walk outside the theater and beat his head against the wall."[27] Probably no one felt concerned enough to bother, because the film was a dismal failure and otherwise went virtually unreported, despite the alluring presence of the contemporary "sex kitten" Mamie Van Doren. Beating up on the beats proved bad business; readers were seeking enlightenment, not putdowns.

Getting Hep to the Beat

For such enlightenment, readers could turn to another journal in New York that was remote from the cloistered academic reviews and was attempting to provide well-publicized outlets for the beats as well as critical interpretations of their aspirations and achievements.

It was launched about the same time that the *Chicago Review* was becoming interested in the San Franciscans; it would last far longer than *Big Table* and would lead to a transplantation of the poetry renaissance to New York. Leroi Jones (later Imamu Amiri Baraka) had become affiliated with the beats when he moved to Greenwich Village in 1957 after serving in the U.S. Air Force and marrying Hettie Cohen, then working for *Record Changer*. He had become an outspoken promoter and defender of the beats.

In March 1958 Leroi and Hettie Jones published the first issue of *Yugen*, which featured works not only by Ginsberg, Corso, and Snyder but also by Burroughs, Charles Olson, and Diane Di Prima, who was to become with Jones a leader of the beat colony in New York. The magazine continued

A Beatnik pad as portrayed in Albert Zugsmith's *The Beat Generation*.
Film still courtesy of Movie Star News, New York.

through eight issues until 1962; in 1961 Di Prima also started a newsletter containing much creative matter, *The Floating Bear,* which she continued to publish for ten years.

Reviewing several published memoirs for the *Village Voice* in 1989, Alix Kates Shulman, a prolific feminist writer, pointedly asked, "Where are the women Beats? Except for poet Diane Di Prima, whose long-out-of-print underground classic, 'Memoirs of a Beatnik' [1969] has now been reprinted, they are hard to find. The tiny handful of women whose work occasionally appears in early Beat anthologies or whose names figure in histories of the period seem to have wandered in from other sensibilities and schools (Denise Levertov, Jean Garrigue . . .)."[28] In a response solicited by the Boulder (Colorado) *Sunday Camera* magazine (in which Shulman's article was reprinted), Allen Ginsberg responded:

Yes, it's all right to blame the men for exploiting the women—or, I think the point is, the men didn't push the women literarily or celebrate them. . . . But then, among the group of people we knew at the time, who were the writers of such power as Kerouac or Burroughs? Were there any? I don't think so.

Were we responsible for the lack of outstanding genius in the women we knew? Did we put them down or repress them? I don't think so. . . .

Where there was a strong writer who could hold her own, like Diane Di Prima, we would certainly work with her and recognize her.[29]

Although some talented women contributed to *Beatitude,* they did not play a large role in San Francisco during the poetry renaissance. (Diane Di Prima was in New York.)

A variant of Shulman's awkward question might be raised about the involvement of blacks and other ethnic minorities. Bob Kaufman, an editor of *Beatitude,* was the only black to contribute substantially to the magazine, and despite the beats' great interest in Oriental art and philosophy, only one native-born Asian, David Rafael Wang, made a significant contribution.

It becomes, therefore, especially ponderable why the leading roles in the New York celebration of the Beat should have been played by a woman and a black man who would subsequently change his lifestyle, his artistic sensibility, and even his name, abandoning the beats, who particularly distrusted ideological commitments and becoming one of the leading activists during the years of ethnic and antiwar protest from 1965 to 1970.

A history of the rapidly changing beat scene on the East Coast during the 1960s would, however, have to cover other elements of the New York literary and art world and thus lies beyond the scope of this western story.

The San Franciscans had to look east not only for good recruits but for the first serious criticism that might give them literary status as something more than sensation-mongers. The initial effort to compile a group of readings that would be helpful in understanding the new sensibility was made by Gene Feldman and Max Gartenberg; their anthology, *The Beat Generation and the Angry Young Men,* was published in 1958 but gained wide circulation only after the appearance of a paperback edition in 1959.

Their editorial viewpoint was that of the internationally minded, young literary trend-seeker in New York (like the editors of *New World Writing*), who was then—as perhaps they always have been—closer to London than to the West Coast of the United States. Feldman and Gartenberg made the only important and perhaps not very appropriate effort to link up the beats with England's Angry Young Men, who had already had a strong impact in the United States through Kingsley Amis's novel *Lucky Jim* (1953), John Osborne's play *Look Back in Anger* (1957), and Colin Wilson's keynote critique, *The Outsider* (1956). The anthologists labeled both groups "new barbarians" who "represent a significant adaptation to life in mid-twentieth century . . . deriving as their rationale an existentialism that suggests Heidegger and Sartre."[30]

Feldman and Gartenberg did concede, however, that there was a "crucial difference" between the two groups: the Britishers "still care," but the Americans were "beyond caring." The Angry Young Men "seek some connection with the world of Insiders, for within that world of false appearances is a truth of social reality. The [beats] completely abjure the Square's world and seek to create a new reality, one in which vivid experience is everything." This analysis led them to the same kind of condescending reductivist view observable in other New York commentators: "The Beat Generation may well suggest a generation of rag pickers looking for Mystery, Magic and God in a bottle, a needle, a horn."[31] Such facile words conjure up memories of the later psychedelic era of the hippies, but they now appear inadequate as a judgment on the beats' complex search for peace and sacrality.

Feldman and Gartenberg's concept of the Beat Generation is curiously narrow and provincial. Of those now regarded as affiliated with the Beat, they included only members of the original New York coterie of the 1940s—Kerouac, Ginsberg, Burroughs, Carl Solomon, and John Clellon Holmes. (Of the other four Americans included—Anatole Broyard, R. V. Cassill, George Mandel, and Chandler Brossard—only Brossard is mentioned in Ann Charters's huge dictionary (*The Beats*), and he is briefly discussed there only to stress that he "does not feel any relationship with the group. . . . 'I have absolutely no affinities with the Kerouac group. They all came 10 years after me. My books were anti-romantic; their work was very romantic, very Huck Finn like.' ")[32] The anthology entirely ignored San Francisco writers, both those from the earlier Rexroth renaissance group and Ferlinghetti, Snyder, and Whalen. Furthermore, all the American selections reprinted, except Ginsberg's *Howl,* without its "Footnote," were from the early 1950s, so that while the anthology provided a compact introduction to some transatlantic tendencies during the decade, it did not really cover the San Francisco Poetry Renaissance.

A later New York effort to take over the beats as a literary property was more promotional than critical. Seymour Krim was a free-lance writer who followed fashions and tried to capitalize upon them but never quite managed to hit the big time. He had begun writing reviews for the *New York Times Book Review* in 1947 and then tried to win acceptance by such highbrow liberal journals as *Hudson Review* and *Partisan Review* by, as Joseph Wenke put it, "meticulously constructing learned articles on modern literature," an undertaking that led to a serious mental breakdown, "after which he began writing about such matters as the breakdown itself."[33] His recovery began just as the beats began making news, and he found their "protest writing, fresh writing, fantastic crazy nutty grim honest liberating fertilizing writing, words and thoughts that come untouched by Madison Avenue's manicured robot hand . . . from the experience we have all shared but been too timid to come out and admit."[34] Thus did he sum up the sentiments of many who had turned to the beats; his anthology *The Beats* provided a good selection from the now established figures—Holmes, Kerouac (excerpts from the still unpublished "Visions of Cody"), Burroughs, Ginsberg, Snyder, Ferlinghetti—as well as from the work of some who had not yet caught on (Richard Barker, Jack Green, Brigid Murnaghan). Claiming that the publisher insisted upon it, Krim also included some critiques, like Podhoretz's. The selection, like other titles from Eastern publishers, was slanted toward New York; Whalen, McClure, and Barbara Moraff were not included, but Diane Di Prima did appear, as well as the reluctant Chandler Brossard, Anatole Broyard, Ted Joans, Hubert Selby, Jr., and Seymour Krim himself ("The Insanity Bit").

On the strength of the success of his beat book, Krim found a publisher for *Views of a Nearsighted Cannoneer* (1961), which carried a backslapping preface by Norman Mailer, after whose *Advertisements for Myself* (1959) Krim had originally modeled these memoirs, which would have consisted of earlier pieces connected by a new running commentary. The original publisher considered the book too long and dropped the commentary, but it was restored for a new edition in 1966.

This debt to Mailer suggests the reason for Krim's failure to maintain the momentum he had generated through a successful (including a Guggenheim Fellowship) but unglamorous teaching career: too much "me-too-ism," presented in a prose that was turgid rather than stimulating. His essay in *The Beats,* for example, opens heavy-handedly, "Until this time of complete blast-off in seemingly every department of human life, the idea of insanity was thought of as the most dreadful thing that could happen to a person."[35] This language is scarcely appropriate for material that was unconventional and still controversial. Krim's talents seem better suited to traditional reviewing, his original trade, than to selling innovative ideas to a skeptical public.

The beats were not dependent, however, on such unpromising newcomers to help them expand their audience. The *Evergreen Review* continued to provide them with an outlet for works that could bear comparison with the best available. The tenth issue (1959), for example, contained the delightful "Tune" by Barbara Moraff, a song for "lots of fresh girl-bodies" ending

"O pluck my twisted bloom,"[36] and Allen Ginsberg's important "Notes Written on Finally Recording *Howl,*" which deflated many obtuse criticisms by patiently explaining that the poem was not simply a spontaneous effusion but "a series of experiments with the formal organization of the long line."[37] Some particularly important additions to the growing beat legacy appeared in the first issue for 1960: Burroughs's "Deposition: Testimony Concerning a Sickness," in which he denounced his fifteen years as a drug addict; Kerouac's "Conclusion of the Railroad Earth," parts of which had appeared before; and Ginsberg's "Sather Gate Illumination," which was inspired by the entrance to the Berkeley campus of the University of California and ends, like the "Footnote" to *Howl,* with a testimony to the "sacrality" of all human life: "Seeing in people the visible evidence of inner self thought by their treatment of me: who loves himself loves me who love [*sic*] myself."[38] This issue also contains "Red-Dirt Marihuana," the first contribution to the review by Terry Southern, who was far too angry to be called a beat but became one of the few celebrated writers of the antiliterate 1960s. His novel *The Magic Christian* was just then being published in the United States, and he was soon to provide the script for the film that became a rallying point for rebellious youth, Stanley Kubrick's *Dr. Strangelove: or, How I Learned to Stop Worrying and Love the Bomb* (1964).

The greatest service that Barney Rosset's Grove Press rendered the beats, however, was not the continued features in the review or its occasional book publication of their works but its sponsoring of Donald M. Allen's *The New American Poetry: 1945–1960.* Many partisans of all kinds of literary tendencies recognized that 1960 was a watershed in America's post–World War II literary history. Several new novelists—John Updike, Philip Roth, James Purdy—who would establish patterns for the future were beginning to publish, and several anthologies of the new poetry of the postwar period appeared during that year. Allen's has proved the most enduring and remains in print, having been revised in 1982.

It was distinctive for making no attempt at comprehensiveness; the editor limited it to what he considered the genuinely "new" voices. He restricted it to poets whom he considered showed some common cause through their relationships with the Black Mountain School, the New York School, or the San Francisco Renaissance (including the beats). This cause, as Allen put it, was "total rejection of all those qualities typical of academic verse" as practiced by the most lauded bards of the time—Theodore Roethke, John Ciardi, Richard Wilbur, Howard Nemerov, Randall Jarrell.

The common influence upon those whom Allen chose was "the practices and precepts of Ezra Pound and William Carlos Williams."[39] Though

probably not all poets included were happy under this banner, they benefited from Allen's tastemaking, particularly among restless college students
and even high schoolers (one of whom was Anne Waldman) who were seeking a way, as Pound had put it, to "make it new." (The admired Pound was,
of course, not the polemicist of the *Cantos* but the early imagist, who had
flourished at the same time as the fauves, seeking to bring into verse the
same kind of stripped-down purity of perception that they brought to their
Collioure paintings.)

Allen's original anthology needs some explication today, for even he was
unable to account fully for the five-part division he made of the selected
poets. The first group were from the Black Mountain School and the third
from the New York School; but it is clear from his arrangement of the San
Francisco poets that he had not, distant as he was from the scene, been able
to sort out the groups to be represented. In the third group of "Beats" he included only Kerouac, Ginsberg, Corso, and Orlovsky. In the second group,
which included contributors like Kenneth Rexroth to the older San Francisco Renaissance, he placed Ferlinghetti (because of his connection with
Rexroth in poetry/jazz programs) and Lew Welch, who, while not present
for much of the poetry renaissance, had even less connection to the older
movement. In a miscellaneous fifth group he placed such beat writers as
Whalen, Snyder, McClure, Stuart Perkoff, Ray Bremser, John Wieners,
Ron Loewinsohn, and David Meltzer, as well as two poets who would be
largely instrumental in bringing the Beat to New York, Leroi Jones and
Gilbert Sorrentino. It was clearly difficult to keep the San Francisco scene in
focus from the other side of the continent (although it is difficult to account
for his omission of Diane Di Prima from any group).[40] Still, his anthology
must be hailed for placing the San Franciscans in the mainstream of American innovative poetry, the mainstream being important to the vitality of any
art. As the fauves along with other bands of painters and poets showed, the
only artists who continue to stand beside the innovators of the present are
the innovators of the past. We lose our sensitivity if we forget them, but we
can only be desensitized by imitators.

Beatitude: Farewell to San Francisco

While the battle over the beats intensified in New York, the poetry renaissance was winding down in San Francisco, as one would have expected
after the *Howl* trial in 1957 vindicated the rights of the beats to share their
vision. Again their situation paralleled that of the fauves, who began to de-
part from Fauvism by the time it had won critical acceptance at the Paris

Salon d'Automne of 1906. As John Elderfield explained, "The focus of their art had radically changed, turning away from landscape and from the joyful celebration of its light and color to something more calculated, conceptual, and classically restrained" (85). Matisse, Derain, and their exuberant associates were never to work in concert again. They were, however, part of a dynamic process of visionary change that led to unprecedented and controversial changes in twentieth-century painting. Once the fauves had established themselves over rival groups as an animating spirit of this change, they had moved on to new concerns, like Braque's cubism, and in the work of Raoul Dufy, who went on to become one of the most important designers and decorators of the century, their vision found a permanent and significant commercial application. So far the only such widely felt impact of the beats had been on Leroi Jones's movement into ethnic activism as Imamu Amiri Baraka—as drastically different an impact on society from Dufy's as can be imagined.

Unlike the fauves, however, the work of the beats was not a crucial turning point in an ongoing dynamic process but—ironically, in view of the title of one of their best-known works—an end of the road. After the beats, literature would never again play the principal shaping role in a visionary attack on the American lifestyle. The hippies, who expressed their psychedelically inspired culture principally through Day-Glo posters and rock music (which have exercised enormous influence on the American sensibility), produced few literary works, and their principal writers—Richard Brautigan, Ken Kesey, Terry Southern, and Richard Fariña—fell, for various reasons beyond the scope of this study, into silence. Before dispersing as the fauves had done, the beats did something that would never have occurred to the French painters: in 1959 a group made an effort to work together on a periodical imbued with the beat spirit.

That spring many of the beats were back in San Francisco. What happened is explained in the introduction to the *Beatitude Anthology:*

The original BEATITUDE magazine was conceived by Allen Ginsberg, Bob Kaufman and John Kelly or someone at Cassandra's coffee house in May 1959 [as a] "weekly miscellany of poetry and other jazz designed to extol beauty and promote the beatific life among the various mendicants, neo-existentialists, christs, poets, painters, musicians and other inhabitants and observers of North Beach, San Francisco, California, United States of America . . . edited on a kick or miss basis by a few hardy types who sneak out of alleys near Grant Avenue—the only responsible party being John Kelly, publisher—offices at 14 Bannam Alley (until tomorrow). . . ." [ellipses in text][41]

Despite the national reputations of Ginsberg, Ferlinghetti, and other contributors, *Beatitude* was not a success. It could not maintain a weekly schedule, and a year after it was started only fifteen issues had appeared. Statements in later issues indicate that even at thirty cents for each mimeographed, usually twenty-four-page copy, the magazine was selling slowly. Archivists ignored it. No research library is listed as possessing a complete file of this publication most intimately connected with writers who have found places in most of the anthologies, histories, and reference guides dealing with contemporary American literature. All that is readily accessible from this slapdash publication, which is uniquely important to American literary history, are the selections of "poetry and other jazz" by forty-one writers that Lawrence Ferlinghetti assembled in 1960 for the 111-page *Beatitude Anthology*, published by his City Lights Books. It is to this that we will turn in the next two chapters to determine just what was communicated on what is called in the anthology "the beat frequency"—to learn what the San Francisco Poetry Renaissance was all about.

With the publication of this anthology, the poetry renaissance was certainly over. By the time it appeared, the anonymous author of the introduction (very likely Ferlinghetti) explained, "Most of the early contributors had made off to faraway scenes and could not be found even to receive their share of the bread produced by the sale of this anthology." In the meantime, a sixteenth issue of *Beatitude* had been produced in exile in New York by new editors. The introduction to the anthology announced that "beginning with issue 17 BEATITUDE will issue spasmodically from the underground caves of City Lights bookstore through whose subterranean passages some of the original BEATITUDE editors may still be reached." But the subsequent issues lacked the vitality of the original ones. The seventeenth made a brave show, with excerpts from Kerouac's *Book of Dreams,* which City Lights was also publishing, along with contributions by Bob Kaufman, Michael McClure, Gregory Corso, David Meltzer, Lenore Kandel, and Ferlinghetti himself and a letter from Leroi Jones, enthusiastic about the prospects for Castro's Cuba. But the eighteenth issue, featuring Gene Fowler's "Fuck Report," was a sad affair, carelessly typed and badly printed.

The beats were, by this time, no longer even an issue in the city. One reason was that, as comments in the *Beatitude Anthology* indicate, people were beginning to find life in North Beach intolerable as the drug culture took hold: some people were unhappy because they could not get drugs or were busted for possession; others were unhappy because the presence of drugs disrupted the community.

The *San Francisco Chronicle* broke the story on 24 January 1960 of Robert Estes, a twenty-nine-year-old private eye who reportedly had spent "five months of life among the beatniks—at marijuana parties, sex orgies and on robbery raids." He was credited by police narcotics officers, for whom he was working undercover, with "providing the key for a roundup of 30 narcotics suspects." A "handsome, crew-cut Army veteran," Estes said, after shaving off his beard and taking "shower after shower," he still did not "feel clean. . . . for my money, they're dirty, they're lazy, they're bums and they're crooks." Matthew O'Connor, chief state narcotics agent in San Francisco, hoped "people realize that we were able to make the arrests because one private citizen gave up his practice . . . for the five months to help us out. We figure he's out about $5,000 in wages in could have made." Not everyone was pleased, however; a Columbus Avenue cafe operator observed, "Most of the beats are decent and well behaved. And they've done more for North Beach than the chamber of commerce and the merchants association combined."[42]

A week later, on 30 January, three hundred beatniks, observed by twenty-five plainclothes policemen, staged a protest in Washington Square against the recent mass marijuana raid. Chester Anderson, an editor of the now-vanished beatnik newspaper *Underhound,* urged the crowd to "stop antagonizing tourists" and "performing for them" and to sue if they were falsely arrested. A student named Jerry Kamstra protested, "I'm tired of being persecuted for not sharing the same social point of view as Officer [William] Bigarani," who the *Chronicle* described as "long a bete noir of the Beatniks." Bigarini was present at the rally but refused to comment.[43]

At a rally the following Saturday, 6 February, Ralph Tyler reported that a larger crowd of four hundred heard a beat spokesman report that "a plan to investigate the 'private and public lives' of Police in North Beach was launched by the Beatniks," who until they could hire detectives would "follow the Police 'beatnik patrol' wherever it goes." Pierre DeLattre of the Bread and Wine Mission said, "The police in North Beach seemed different from those in other areas. . . . Gestapo-type atmosphere has been created there."[44] A protest rally was announced for the next weekend at the state capitol at Sacramento.

Whatever the merits of the cases presented by the opponents in this confrontation, people were beginning to find North Beach life untenably contentious. The one anonymous entry in the *Beatitude Anthology* was a parody of *Howl,* beginning

> I saw the best mind of North Beach beat with a bagel,
> stupid, histrionic, numbrained

> dragging itself through the coffee shops at eve
> looking for an angry thunderbird
> Richard De Rimer I'm with you in Mexico. . . .

It was described as having been read at "a 'Get Rid of De Rimer Night' conceived by the poet himself as a means of getting to Mexico [by convincing] wealthy citizens that De Rimer was the sort who must, out of civic duty, be sent away. Improvised poems were recited to stimulate distaste, among them this one by a priest and a rabbi."[45]

Jory Sherman reported on the situation during the last week of April 1960:

Alan Dienstag and C. V. J. Anderson are feuding over UNDERHOUND policy or something. Dienstag may just turn the whole thing over to Chet. Also one of the editors of BEATITUDE . . . absconded with 500 bucks of the money, and worse, the entire subscription list. . . . Aaron [Miller] just came back from Venice [California] where he had stayed for a couple of weeks, and said it was completely dead . . . and that there is the real beatnik haven. So I lost interest right there.

The others are pretty much the same as I am. We hate Grant Ave., but we still go there, and there is [*sic*] possibilities of filtering out serious artists from the bums. It is wonderful when you can walk down and talk to people like Vincent McHugh, and James Broughton and Richard McBride . . . [and] others, so nice and warm, serious people.[46]

Nothing came of the scheme to filter out the bums. Sherman later reported, "I don't know what is going to happen on North Beach, but I do know a lot of real artists are sick of it. . . . Alan Dienstag is, Pierre deLattre, Chet Anderson, Al Clemente [a photographer], and on and on. . . . They are spreading out and finding places far far from Grant Avenue." He also praised the vitality of Ruth Weiss.[47]

At the same time a *Gemini* correspondent pointed out that Kenneth Rexroth had disowned the beats.[48] His opposition, however, lacked any significant force. It is sad to read, mercilessly printed in their entirety, the rambling remarks that he made over Pacifica radio station KFPA in Berkeley on 13 August 1960. Reaching what should have been the climax of his attack on "The Commercialization of the Image of Revolt," he lost his grip on his subject when he turned to "the kind of spuriously disengaged literature that has become popular. . . . So, if this is worn out (and I certainly think it is; it has sunk to the lowest pocketbook level), what is going to take its place? I don't know. I'm always asked this by students. They say, 'Well, what should we do, you know? What should we join? What should we write?'

And I always say, 'Well, you're twenty and I'm fifty. You tell me.' . . . I don't think there's any party book that will solve [the great besetting problems of society] all automatically.' " He lamely observed, "I should think that we can no longer afford alienation."[49]

Even local businesspeople had ceased to be encouraging. One of the landmarks of the beat/beatnik community had been Jay Hoppe's Co-existence Bagel Shop at the corner of Grant Avenue and Green Street. In April 1960 a local nuisance identified only as "Mad Marie" had hit Hoppe in the chest with a brick, and the police had hauled *him* in. That September his once flourishing business lost $1500. On 12 October he shut up shop. He blamed the police: "I am tired of having to deal with a sick city administration and a psychopathic police department. I am tired of San Francisco and I never want to see it again."[50]

Others shared his sentiments and those of Philip Whalen:

> Almost all Americans aged 4 to 100
> Have the spiritual natures of Chicago policemen.
> Scratch an American and find a cop. There is no
> Generation gap.[51]

Chapter Three

Downbeat

Despite all that has been written about the Beat Generation, one problem that has never been resolved is just what the word *beat* means in this context. When the term was supposedly coined by Jack Kerouac in the 1940s, the character (Gene Pasternak) who is his alter ego in John Clellon Holmes's novel *Go,* used it to suggest what Kenneth Rexroth later called "the art of the Beat Generation"—disengagement. Early in the novel, Pasternak observes, "You know, everyone I know is kind of furtive, kind of beat. They all go along the street like they were guilty of something, but didn't believe in guilt" (36).

Kerouac used *beat* only ten times in *On the Road,* and on each occasion the word carried the sense of something or someone who has been defeated by the world, though without any personal responsibility for the defeat. The word first appears in section 3 of part I, when Sal Paradise (Kerouac's self-portrait), on his first attempt to hitchhike across the country, joins forces with a New York Irishman: "He was a real rednose drunk of thirty. . . . He wore a *beat* sweater and baggy pants and had nothing with him in the way of a bag—just a toothbrush and handkerchiefs" (emphasis added).[1] Later Sal speaks more specifically of those "rising from the underground, the sordid hipsters of America, a new beat generation that I was slowly joining" (54). The term acquires another shade of meaning at the climax of part III, in the description of Dean Moriarty's (Neal Cassady) wild driving from California to Chicago. Sal, who is becoming increasingly disillusioned with Dean, finally finds the words to describe him: "That's what Dean was, the HOLY GOOF" (194). When Dean is confronted by accusations from former friends, Sal notes that "where once [he] would have talked his way out, he now fell silent. . . . He was BEAT—the root, the soul of Beatific" (195). A few pages earlier, Sal explained the change that has overcome Dean, as he sees him one morning standing naked at the window, "looking at all San Francisco . . . as the sun came up. . . . He looked like some day he'd be the pagan mayor of San Francisco. But his energies ran out" (175). What has fascinated many readers of the novel is the characters' drive, the raw energy—like the energy that fueled the fauves' achievement. But when this energy is exhausted, the characters are *beat,* left at the mercy of an insensitive world, like "the best minds of my generation" in Ginsberg's *Howl.*

It is this conception of the beat, however, that ultimately enraged Kenneth Rexroth. When the outlanders seemed to be taking over his carefully nurtured renaissance, he complained, "The disengagement of the creator, who, as creator, is necessarily judge is one thing, but the utter nihilism of the emptied-out hipster is another. What is going to come of an attitude like this? It is impossible to go on indefinitely saying, 'I am proud to be a delinquent,' without destroying all civilized values." He had forebodings that the result of the hipster position would be "the desperation of shipwreck—the despair, the orgies, ultimately the cannibalism of a lost lifeboat."[2] Rexroth's prediction does chillingly foreshadow Kerouac's breakdown as fictionalized in *Big Sur* and the ultimate self-destructions of both Kerouac and Neal Cassady.

But Rexroth's unchanging attitude—that the beats were motivated only by their uncompromisingly nihilistic rejection of the world—indicated only how far he had himself become disengaged from the group he originally fostered once he thought that they had sold out for commercial success. In an article published the same year in *Esquire,* "The Philosophy of the Beat Generation," John Clellon Holmes attempted to counter this simplistic reductivism. He explained that critics of *On the Road*

spent so much time expressing their polite distaste for the sordidness of some of the material, that they completely failed to mention that in . . . the world of the Beat Generation, Kerouac unfailingly found tenderness, humility, joy, and even reverence. . . . Whatever else they may be, these are not the words of a generation consumed by self-pity over the loss of their illusions; nor are they the words of a generation consumed by hatred for a world they never made. They seem rather to be the words of a generation groping toward faith out of an intellectual despair and moral chaos in which they refuse to lose themselves.[3]

Partisan Holmes, however, seemed somewhat too finicky when he stressed the beats' break with the formalities of their university-imprisoned forebears but in the same paragraph described Ginsberg's meticulously constructed *Howl* as "disordered."

It took one of the despised academics, Thomas Parkinson of Berkeley, to reject gossip columnist Herb Caen's cynical identification of the beats with the beatniks. In *A Casebook on the Beat,* he agreed that "it was easy to deride the nonconformist existential costumes, the sheer unpleasantness of texture in the dreary fakeries of beatnik art, and [that] no one could defend the aimless self-destructiveness and occasional pointless criminality of conduct." But Parkinson objected to confusing these characters with "the genuine vigor and force of Allen Ginsberg and Jack Kerouac, the extraordinary wit and hilarity of Lawrence Ferlinghetti and Gregory Corso, the obvious intelligence, learning and decency of Gary Snyder and Philip Whalen, the hard integrity of Michael McClure—in short, the simple literary expertise of several gifted writers who participated in many of the excitements and obsessions of current Bohemia" (270).

Although he recognized and celebrated the craftsmanship and dedication of the beats, Parkinson was less helpful in descrying just where their concerns lay because he perceived them in relation to a still tradition-directed society. He pointed out that the "true radicals" of the preceding New Deal generation "went on to formulate [their] motives in terms of some ideal mode of social organization." "But the beat movement," he continued, "simply denied the role of the social critic and took an indifferent and passive posture before the problems of the world. . . . With very few exceptions, the beat and beatnik compose a social refusal rather than a revolt. . . . They take no particular pleasure in tearing down a social fabric that they see as already ruined, and their attitude toward society is suspicious and evasive rather than destructive" (277). Where he parted company with the beats is marked by his statement that, "in truth, there is a vast fund of good sense and social responsibility in this country, and the only problem is to allow its voice to be heard more clearly and loudly" (279). If he was right, that voice has yet to make itself heard over the clamor generated by self-seeking messiahs and the shrill voices of hucksters seeking to stimulate consumer dissatisfaction and create new wants.

What Parkinson, as a representative of his generation and of his once genteel calling, had been conditioned to find difficult to perceive was the beats' lack of belief in any "ideal mode of social organization," although such skepticism was no new thing in the 1950s: the beats were exponents of Thoreau's view in "Civil Disobedience" that "government at best is but an expedient."[4] Parkinson was too sentimentally conditioned to grasp the concept of "beat" as "a declaration of unconditioned mind . . . beyond winner or loser." The beats did not believe in accepting anything on faith and especially did not believe in committing oneself to somebody else's utopian fantasies like "the kid" Philip Whalen mentioned who "put it clear as may be: / 'I want America to be magic electrical Tibet.'" Sometime later in the same work Whalen quickly disposed of two of the great revolutionary impulses that have inspired many: "The American Revolution was a tax-dodge / Dreamed up by some smart Harvard men / . . . Russian Revolution a strictly ugly downtown proposition / The Great Unwashed on a rampage. . . ."[5] In his poem that provided the keynote for the *Beatitude Anthology*, Whalen, like "the kid," stated the beat position as clearly as possible: "I renounce the notion of all social responsibility."

A Divided Sensibility: Alternate Frequencies

Even such an all-inclusive rejection as Whalen's need not be taken, however, as the monolithic viewpoint underlying all the creations that can be called "beat." Even those artists who accept the idea that one cannot hope to change the world to suit one's own desires can be divided into two general, interrelated groups: those who express a despairing, even nihilistic and apocalyptic vision (which was especially popular after World War II) of society being desperate and beyond repair, so that the end of this ill-conceived world seems likely, if not in fact desirable; and those, in accordance with the precepts of Whitman and Thoreau, with the vision to try to adjust to the situation and make the most of inescapable chaos, since, as Wallace Stevens put it in "A Glass of Water," "In a village of the indigenes, / One would have still to discover."

Indeed, what one finds on closely comparing the poems selected for the *Beatitude Anthology* is that they illustrate exactly such a division. Being able to discern these two "frequencies," one can label them, with almost embarrassing banality, "downbeat" and "upbeat."

Philip Whalen, as we shall see, exemplified most often in his work an upbeat viewpoint. His renunciation of "social responsibility" was a fresh and timely restatement of the attitude that Thoreau expressed in *Walden* toward "do-gooders": "If I knew for certain that a man was coming to my house with the conscious design of doing me good, I should run for my life . . . for fear that I should get some of his good done to me."

On the other hand, most of the statements that we have examined so far in this chapter by Jack Kerouac and by critics of the beats, have been derived from the downbeat perspective, which not only dominated most of Kerouac's fiction but is too often accused of having infected all of beat "philosophy" with defeatism.

Thus, it has often gone unnoticed that the generation as a whole and what is widely acknowledged as its outstanding creation, *Howl,* stand *between* downbeat and upbeat and illustrate both the gap and the possible bridge between the two positions.

Howl closely resembles in its formal ambiguity another imposing work at the watershed between two cultural eras—Mozart's opera *Don*

Giovanni which can be performed either with or without a cautionary epilogue that follows the tremendous scene of the Don's damnation. If the epilogue is used, the opera seems to be one of the last great statements of the neoclassic era, portraying the vulgar upstart Don's paroxysmal behavior in order at last to condemn it and warn against its imitation by others; if the epilogue is omitted, as it frequently has been in recent years, the libretto can be interpreted as the tragedy of a doomed outsider crushed by a stiflingly proper society.[6] *Howl* reverses these impressions: without its "Footnote" it can be read as a hopeless overflowing of feelings of despair and doom, but with it added, as Ginsberg seems to have intended and as Mark Schorer assumed, the poem suggests a possible salvation from the Goyaesque horrors of the earlier strophes. This salvation would be found, however, not in "religion" (which suggests the very institutionalized practice that the poem and the beats denounce) but in "sacrality," a way of living that is free of sectarian conditioning and that views each object and experience as unique and holy.

This discrimination of two streams in the beat impulse suggests that even in a rebellion that rejects ideological commitment, two long-continuing and opposing visions are possible: the primitivistic and the progressive theories of the human condition. The former looks back to an imagined better time in the past and sees human history as a devolution toward an impending apocalypse; the latter looks forward from present despair to a better future (but not necessarily the cultists' promised state of perfection) and sees human history as evolutionary—if sometimes a frustratingly slow process. (Contrast, for example, William Faulkner's "Delta Autumn" with John Steinbeck's statement in Chapter 14 of *The Grapes of Wrath*.) To analyze the presence of one or both of these streams in the works of the beat writers would require separate studies of each individual; but a convenient vehicle for launching an investigation of these tendencies in the beats is the *Beatitude Anthology*.

The anthology is made up of three groups of writings, mostly poems, which we are told are "not all on the beat frequency." Most selections reflect either negative or positive alternations of the same current, but another smaller group seems to be broadcasting from beyond the beat spectrum. The two larger groups may be labeled "downbeat" and "upbeat"; the remainder are "offbeat."

Although the three groups of writings are not rigorously segregated, there are evidences of a deeper plan behind the ordering of the selections, possibly related to Ferlinghetti's enthusiasm for "street" poetry. The contents move from the seemingly most spontaneous and unaffected (in Peter

Orlovksy's street poems the previous editors' "corrected spellings" have been replaced by his original, "more poetic" ones) through steadily more artful forms to Robert Stock's intricate villanelle and a collection of traditional haiku. The opening selections (closest to the street) are predominantly downbeat, but the poems tend to lighten as their forms become more demanding. Let us begin—as both the anthology and this discussion do—with the downbeat.

Laments of the Lovers

It is doubtful that anyone but Orlovsky's close friends have found much merit in his poetic efforts (Thomas Parkinson entirely ignored him), and Ferlinghetti indulged a malicious wit in starting the collection with three of Orlovsky's distinctly "street" and downbeat effusions. The opening selections from *Subway*, and "Morris," his longest contribution, could exemplify "unconditioned mind," for there is an intriguing discrepancy between the first-person narrators in these poems and the depressing world they observe. In "Subway 2" the narrator sits "silent but happy bound / that all my New York family is here."[7] At the end of "Morris," when the narrator, a night attendant in a mental hospital, observes the helpless title character "wet again," he does not scold but simply obliges—"just a minite I'll get a new set of pajamers"—and advises Morris to "Love everybody" (14). But not only does the narrator admit that "There are no clean cut rules for saving Morris" (10), who has "got paranoia" (3), but also all the "family" he meets in the subway are "sad . . . straightfaced & mummy fixed" (7). Orlovsky's vignettes all seem drawn from what Ferlinghetti called "a gone world."

The period when *Beatitude* was being published in San Francisco seems to have found Ginsberg in sad shape. He was still suffering greatly from the death of his mother. His contributions—the largest group in the book, seven poems running eleven of the 111 pages—begin with the "Hymn" from "Kaddish," written in her memory. Another poem is his version of one by Liang Kai of China's Southern Sung dynasty and ends with one of the rare references in the volume to "beatness," here identified as "humility . . . before the absolute World" (19).

Ginsberg was also about to undertake a disastrous season of experiments with psychedelic drugs under Timothy Leary. Such experimentation was the occasion for "Mescaline," which finds the speaker preoccupied with thoughts of death:

> Yes, I should be good, I should get married
> find out what it's all about
> but I can't stand these women all over me . . .
> can't stand boys even anymore. (16)

Almost in direct contrast to the "Footnote" to *Howl,* this poem ends, "No point writing when the spirit doth not lead" (18). A series of impressions in "Afternoon Seattle" come into focus in an ultra-beat statement, in Kerouac's original downbeat sense: "The cities rot from the center, the suburbs fall apart / a slow apocalypse of rot the spectral trolleys fade" (20).

Gloomiest of all, however, is "Over Kansas," the longest meditation of the group, which is launched with the question, "Where shall I fly / not to be sad, my dear?" (21). Although the traveler notes that a few moments have been brightened by gorgeous young men, his dominant feeling recurs in the reflection that provides the poem's title: "Travelling thru the dark void / over Kansas yet moving nowhere / in the dark void of the soul" (23). The whole group of poems is on a very downbeat frequency, which Ginsberg analyzes himself in a poem about writing poems, "On Visions," written in 1953. He ends his reflections on the work of visionaries whose quests for the sublime have inspired him in the past by ". . . inquiring what / harvest consumed in the substance / of the withered decades / ripens in my imagination" (25). In a letter to John Kelly at the end of the anthology, Peter Orlovsky notes that Allen's "not writ much" (110).

The anthology does not include any of Kerouac's poems; three selections from his *Book of Dreams,* which City Lights was getting ready to publish, are reprinted. *Book of Dreams* is an irritating work because the nocturnal visitations that Kerouac tried to set down as soon as he woke are neither dated nor put in any context. They are generally quite downbeat. In the first one reprinted in the anthology, he is being chased by a "cow-goat" that "is taking tragic Pink Chagall bites out of me" (26), and in the third one he is chased by cops before he goes into "a beat bar" and starts some unresolved haggling over price with a "blond whore" (28). The second selection is a long shared nightmare and is one of the grimmest anticommunist pieces out of a number included in *Book of Dreams.* Kerouac is part of group of one hundred, including Cody (Neal Cassady), being held captive, until he is spirited away from the "Firingsquad Photographers" to be the sex slave of the prison's "women cooks & waitresses who need man-love so badly that they have developed a super secret subterranean system of . . . sumptuous underground lovemaking apartments" (27).

Other Roads Down

Another twelve contributors, just half of those who can be assigned to one of the two principal beat frequencies, were on the same one as Kerouac and Ginsberg. Three of them—Corso, McClure, and Lamantia—had also been involved in the first group reading at the Six Gallery in 1955. Since their works are grouped near the beginning of the book, anyone reading them consecutively feels pretty beat down before getting much relief.

The first was Gregory Corso, who had happened into poetry while serving a prison term for robbery. After his release in 1950, he met Kerouac and Ginsberg in New York, where they undertook his reeducation. Despite his closeness to the founding beats, Corso, as Marilyn Schwartz observed, has been "almost totally disregarded by serious reviewers," who have found his pyrotechnical verse (for instance, "Bomb" and "Gasoline") flashy rather than solid.[8] Parkinson thought Corso's "stock in trade is impertinence" (280), though he did include in the *Casebook* an early essay on Corso's work by Carolyn Gaiser. She admitted that "he seems to have built-in sense of form that protects him from embarrassingly sloppy writing," but she accused Kerouac and Ginsberg, "as might be expected," of most "vociferously" praising "the least disciplined and the least successful, such as 'Bomb' and 'Power.' "[9] The ambiguous poem "One Day," his single contribution to the *Beatitude Anthology,* somewhat resembles Orlovsky's longer *Subway;* the narrator, "Peter-Panning the sky" (one of the catchy phrases that most attracted attention to Corso and are probably the charm of his works) and a seemingly carefree soul, encounters a dying man. After a dolorous interchange in which the dying man observes, "The sky is awful!" the narrator departs and the man dies, as he "must always . . . for Solitude refuses to lower a gentle hand / upon his long sad face" (31).

The *Beatitude* year seems also to have witnessed a flagging of Michael McClure's usually abundant energies. He was represented in the anthology only by "Lines from a Peyote Depression." In 1958, McClure recalled in *Scratching the Beat Surface,* he had his first vivid experience with peyote buttons, which he described in "Peyote Poem." In those days, he wrote, drugs "were taken for joy, for consciousness, for spiritual elevation," and he found the experience exhilarating: "THIS IS THE POWERFUL KNOWLEGE / we smile with it."[10] By the time he wrote "Lines from a Peyote Depression," however, a reaction had set in; it begins, "((THERE IS NO TIME OF LOVE IN PAIN OF LOVE OR FACES {IN THE AIR. SEE / I call them and they do not come," and reaches its climax in the repeated use of the word *COLD* followed by "{AND FAR AWAY" (31–32).

Although Philip Lamantia was one of the readers at the Six Gallery in 1955 (where he read John Hoffman's poems) and a contributor to *Beatitude,* he is usually regarded as an onlooker rather than a participant in the Beat Generation. He had been prominent in San Francisco among the Rexroth group before the beats had appeared, winning a reputation as a surrealist with his first book of poems in 1946. But he was largely inactive, as Rexroth complained, during the poetry renaissance, and did not publish another book until 1959. Many of his poems are difficult to follow because of his free association techniques and heavy use of allusions, many of them obscure. "Füd at Foster's" is no exception, although its relation to the beats is apparent from Lamantia's use of the term "reality sandwiches," which Ginsberg later used for a collection of his works from the period. Lamantia's use, however, suggests revulsion, with its emphatic "NO MORE REALITY SANDWICHES." There follows a series of increasingly hysterical questions, ending with, "Can I sit on the Moon?" The increasing anger and despair of the poem is framed by the lines, "Junk's unlimited and sold by Agents," and, "the jails are too small, sweaty AND STINK" (33). The tone resembles McClure's, in stark contrast to their joyous evening's association in 1955. Like much else in *Beatitude,* the poems of McClure and Lamantia convey a sense of a winding down of energies like that depicted in *On the Road.*

Lamantia's poem also seems closely related to the only one by a writer identified only as "Marc," who in "Mexico 5 '59" describes a very unpleasant trip to Mazatlán after a "very keen" party the night before "blowing khif and chewing buttons." After arriving in the Mexican city he meets "a man named Harry," but then says nothing more besides, "it was very cold there" (40).

Father DeLattre's Mission

This repeated presentation of a world that is not at all "cool" in the hipster sense but downright cold is continued in a poem by an individual very important to the poetry renaissance, not so much for his own creative work as for the comfort and encouragement he offered the community, especially through his Bread and Wine Mission, where the beats congregated and for a time printed *Beatitude.*

Pierre Henri DeLattre was a formally trained Congregational minister who wished to become a creative writer. But as he explained, "I wanted to have something to write about; so, I decided to spend the first 10–20 years of my life involved in social action, trying to encourage what I thought was a very important movement, the counter culture." He began publishing poems early in the 1950s in *Golden Goose* and other little magazines. Then he came to North Beach in the late 1950s as a street priest; there he dealt with "many casualities . . . a lot of the experience of the Beat Generation was one of picking up the pieces."[11] He also held services and performed marriages, and at the height of public fascination with the beats his mission was written up in *Time* and *Newsweek*.[12] He did not, however, have high hopes for beat writing. "I think that it is an insignificant force," he told interviewers in 1981.[13] By 1965 he had become a Buddhist and moved to San Miguel Allende, Mexico, where there was a sizable American expatriate colony, because he did not want to pay taxes to support the Vietnam War. He became head of the writing department at the Allende Institute and began to concentrate on his own writings, placing poems not only in little magazines but in academic reviews like the University of Nebraska's *Prairie Schooner* and *Carleton Miscellany*. He published two books of fiction, the whimsical *Tales of a Dalai Lama* (1971) and a touching fable about circus tightrope walkers, *Walking on Air* (1982).

His contribution to the *Beatitude Anthology*, though a rather prosy poem, shows a rare mixture of traditional compassion with contemporary awareness. "Woman in a Bohemian Bar" is a complex reverie, contrasting the speaker's adolescent sexual fantasies with a disillusioningly matter-of-fact maturity as he contemplates a woman he suspects of having a death wish. Her emotional descent lands her in a honky-tonk bar, to which she reacts with terror. "If she could know love," the speaker muses, "I would proclaim / An exit from the tomb," and he could cease "This daily walk of fear" (67). *If* is the controlling word that makes this a downbeat poem, for the speaker sees no prospect that this woman he often watches could ever break through the wall around her to realize that everything is holy, as Allen Ginsberg prays in the "Footnote" to *Howl*.

Father DeLattre's narrator worries about the woman he helplessly observes rather than himself. The downbeat image, however, that many contributors cultivated is most depressingly displayed in a group of poems by B. (Berne) Uronovitz, one of the editorial helpers on *Beatitude*. The speaker in "The Sacrifice" describes himself as "another superfluous man" (48), and the one in "A Possible Panacea" wonders whether "a well- / placed bullet / Might not clear my mind / Of these terrible / neural disorders" (51). Alan Dienstag, an editor of *Underhound*, exemplified what Thomas Parkinson considered "beatnik work" in his poems about four women who made intolerable demands: in "Where Love Has Gone Love," the speaker's "quicksand bed / Is dying of hunger" (69).

Women's Voices

So far all of the contributions cited from the *Beatitude Anthology* have been by men, and indeed, we reach page 70, almost two-thirds of the way through the book, before the first woman's voice is heard. Poems by eight women are then grouped together in a seventeen-page section, effectively separating the preceding "street" poets from the last section of male writers whose work displays somewhat more traditional tendencies. (One can make of this arrangement what one will.)

As has been acknowledged in the previous chapter, women writers did not figure prominently in the North Beach scene, although one can wonder why they made a relatively larger proportional contribution to individual issues of *Beatitude* than is reflected by their representation in the anthology. The poems by women that were chosen for inclusion in the anthology are also more concerned with heterosexual lovemaking than those by the men chosen.

Only three of the women's works can be called downbeat, and these are not grouped together. In Anne Frost's "Chippie's Lament," the title character "took a bad train to bad places" because she had been "exiled / From Johnny the Bonny / Leaving true love behind me" (75). Ruth Weiss, a frequent contributor to *Beatitude* and one of the most active and dynamic members of the community, is represented by "Poem," a less personal but equally downbeat picture of a city occupied by hungry animals from the hills after it has been deserted by human inhabitants (87).

The most spectacularly downbeat of the women was Lenore Kandel, who would subsequently—after even the hippies were following the beats out of town—be involved in the last highly publicized case of attempted censorship by the city's police. A native of New York who had lived in Los Angeles and San Francisco earlier, she arrived back in the Bay Area in 1960, already an established poet with three books published in southern California to her credit. The poetry renaissance was winding down, but she made it in time to become involved in an affair with Lew Welch, which won her dubious fame as the model for Ramona Schwartz, "that big brunette . . . Rumanian madwoman," in Jack Kerouac's novel *Big Sur* (she was actually of Russian-Turkish ancestry) and to contribute to *Beatitude*.[14] Her "First They Slaughtered the Angels" is one of the most striking poems in the collection—a kind of feminist *Howl* that raises the same kind of questions as Ginsberg's epic:

> who finked on the angels?
> who stole the holy grail and hocked it for a jug of wine? . . .

who barbecued the lamb of god? . . .
who raped St. Mary with a plastic dildo stamped with the
Good Housekeeping seal of approval?

The answer is the "androgynes" in the "alleyways," who "have denied both christ and cock" and "nominated a eunuch for president," shouting, "Lobotomy for the houswife! / Lobotomy for the business man! / Lobotomy for the nursery schools!" (80). Despite this downbeat picture of a wasted world, Kandel ends not with Ginsberg's plea for sacrality but with the cry of an underground activist: "we shall enter into the streets and walk among them and do battle" (83).

She would become best known for *The Love Book* (1966), the first book she published in San Francisco. It consists almost entirely of repetitions of the word *fuck* arranged in various patterns on the pages. After it went on sale, clerks at the Psychedelic Shop in Haight-Ashbury and (once more) Ferlinghetti's City Lights Bookshop (thus linking hippies and beat survivors) were arrested for "pandering to obscenity." Although Kandel testified at the trial that the book was the "culmination of a 23-year search for an appropriate way to worship the divinity of man and express her belief that sexual acts between loving persons are religious acts," the prosecution reviled it as "animalistic," "blasphemous," "psychiatrically immature," "odious," and "excessive and nauseating."[15] After five weeks the defendants were found guilty, but the verdict was overturned on appeal. Kandel made little attempt to capitalize on the publicity that she had received and published only one more collection of poems, *Word Alchemy* (1967). Since then she has dropped out of sight—her biographer Donna Nance thinks deliberately, and regrettably—though in *Outsider 4&5* (1969) she reported that she was living and working in Hawaii.

Bob Kaufman and Abomunism

Kandel's history of unusual activism for a beat affiliate, followed by withdrawal from activism when it became more fashionable, provides a clue to the even stranger career of one of the most inscrutable and by some critics most admired figures connected with the poetry renaissance.

Bob Kaufman was conspicuous to begin with—he was the only black writer to be prominently associated with *Beatitude*. Born in New Orleans in 1925, he was a contemporary of the readers at the Six Gallery in 1955, slightly older than Ginsberg and Snyder but younger than Philip Whalen. He spent twenty years in the U.S. Merchant Marine, which he had entered at thirteen. During this service he met Ginsberg and Burroughs in New York during the 1940s, but he did not meet Kerouac and Neal Cassady until the 1950s, when he moved to California and married. His first published work, *The Abomunist Manifesto* (1959), appeared from City Lights Books as a broadside after it had appeared serially in *Beatitude* as one of the magazine's few prose features.

By its very nature as a manifesto, this mock-serious document is one of the least typically beat works in the anthology; yet its opening statement— "ABOMUNISTS join nothing but their hands or legs, or other same" (57) —clearly expresses the essence of the feelings shared by this nonbinding confederation. At the same time that it burlesques the manifestos of other groups who loudly denounced bourgeois conformity while insisting on strict adherence to a party line (the surrealists under the authoritarian André Breton were especially noted for issuing proclamations and excommunicating heretics), it slyly articulates a credo for those who do not believe in credos or institutionalized thought and action.

Kaufman's manifesto is also one of the few attempts at humor from *Beatitude.* Although the beats often talked about "joy," they did not find life funny; it was too full of horrors, and the desperately sought joy was found only fitfully. (As we shall see, Richard Brautigan's early poems seemed out of place in *Beatitude.*) Satire likewise was rarely found in the beats' work because it is ultimately grounded in the acceptance of those very sociopolitical norms that rebels seek to displace when a society loses its integrity. Satire seeks reform, not Kerouac's "unconditioned mind beyond protest."

Bob Kaufman, however, strained to make his fourteen-point manifesto satirical. It is accompanied by a "lexicon" of twenty-seven terms that begins provincially: "ABOMMUNITY. n. Grant Avenue & other frinky places" (58). The third proviso in the manifesto is that "Abomunists do not look at pictures painted by presidents and unemployed prime ministers" (57)—a dig at the "Sunday paintings" of Eisenhower and Churchill. Kaufman's document resembles Ferlinghetti's "Tentative Description of a Dinner Given to Promote the Impeachment of President Eisenhower" (which attracted even the attention of J. Edgar Hoover, to whom the U.S. Secret Service replied that the author "may possibly be a mental case").[16] Kaufman's protest, however, lacked the aging Kerouac's caustic bitterness in his denunciation of Columbia College's course in contemporary civilization.[17]

The emphasis throughout Kaufman's work is not on disengagement but on an oppressive society's rejection of reformers. In "Notes" on Abomunism[11] he turned to the overworked idea of a beat transfiguration of Christ in a translation of "the live sea scrolls": Christ, counting down the days to the end of "B.C.," says, "I was framed," and ends, "What a drag" (60–62). This is followed by Ferlinghetti's "Loud Prayer," which begins, "Our father whose art's in heaven / hollow be thy name" (62).

Besides the Abomunist materials, the *Beatitude Anthology* also includes thirty-five stanzas of "Jail Poems," making Kaufman's contribution the second longest in the book, almost as long as Ginsberg's. "Jail Poems" also dwell on the idea of rejection, but again, not so much the speaker's rejection of the world, as in *Howl,* but the world's rejection of the speaker. Not only are we told, in poem IV, that "Mr. America . . . will help kill me. / He probably hates beatniks" (52), but also, in poem XIV, that after "All the Jews were burned, artists all destroyed," Adolph Hitler became bored, "So he moved to San Francisco, became an ordinary / Policeman, devoted himself to stamping out Beatniks" (54).

Kaufman was the only writer in the collection to make frequent use of the word *beatnik.* Although Kaufman was one of the founders of *Beatitude,* his position was far more militant than that of most of the beats, and he probably had sound reasons for writing of himself as a beatnik. In fact, his work is useful for distinguishing between beat and beatnik on the basis of the latter's narcissistic preoccupation with self in contrast to the former's commiserating contemplation of others' distresses. (This distinction could characterize such late works of Kerouac as *Vanity of Duluoz* as beatnik, and this characterization could be useful in distinguishing the very different treatment by these works of events also fictionalized in some earlier novels, such as *The Town and the City.*) Kaufman also appeared in 1959 in a film made by the distinguished English critic Kenneth Tynan, *Dissent in the Arts in America,* which has never been shown in the United States because of objections from the House of Representatives Committee on Un-American Activities, though it has been popular in Europe. (Kaufman's work is also better known in Europe than in the United States.) He might have been expected to join Leroi Jones in active black militancy during the 1960s, but in one of his most extraordinary actions after the death of President John F. Kennedy he took a Buddhist vow of silence and maintained it for twelve years—until after the end of the Vietnam War.

His long silence largely accounted for his being forgotten in the rapid shifts of the American avant-garde. After making a few appearances in the mid-1970s, he abruptly renounced writing and withdrew into solitude again in 1978; but he again gave a few readings after 1982 before his death in 1986. A. D. Winans wrote an extraordinarily discerning and sympathetic article about Kaufman that avoids the excesses of the beat's own writing while perhaps not being tough enough on his shortcomings. Winans felt that Kaufman deserved long overdue critical acclaim and praised especially his ability "to move from anger to humor in a matter of seconds."[18] But even this characteristic illustrates an extreme instability in Kaufman's behavior. Furthermore, writing that can change quickly to hysteria and that attracts attention abroad as a manifestation of an American syndrome was not limited to the beats, nor was it even characteristic of them. Kaufman can be remembered as the most outstanding of the beatniks; he lived his life as a protest but never transmuted it into an art comparable to Ginsberg's or Ferlinghetti's.

Down, Down into the Grave

The kind of hysteria that underlies Kaufman's work is present as a subtext from the beginning and persists to the end of the downbeat selections in the *Beatitude Anthology.* The less shrill of Raymond Samuel Meyerbach's two contributions, "Local 1," presents a speaker taking the same boldly defiant stance as Lenore Kandel; he announces, "The poets' union . . . is on strike against the world," then promises, "By God," that he will "march au naturel through heav'n." But the mood of the accompanying "Death Poem" is a complete turnaround. It depicts a Warsaw rabbi "conducting his service to an empty synagogue as [death's] bullets shatter the night," an image that leaves the speaker "afraid" (93).

Few such holocaust images occur in the anthology; the fear assaulting the beats was of American origin. Richard McBride makes this clear when, urging a son to run away in "Deathman," the speaker warns, "Here he comes / Putting his / Atomic Finger / On / Your dreams' doorbell" (94).

In the much more frightening poem that precedes this one in the book, Jory Sherman takes us to "White Sands," the atomic testing grounds in New Mexico, to discover for "lovers" the message that it is "Better to weep the agonies of the lonely! / than strike babes to a haze of bloodqueer; / see them eaten blue in a vein of ant fangs / fat as careless mushrooms sick" (92). Sherman is not among those memorialized in Ann Charters's *The Beats.* But this poem, like those in the chapbook *So Many Doors,* also published in 1960, suggests that this newcomer, who was to have taken over the editorship of *Beatitude,* might have carried on the distinctly beat tradition of Ginsberg, Corso, and McClure. He had to support a large family, however, and turned to writing western romances—often under pseudonyms—for a German audience that still enjoys them.

Most nearly on the downbeat frequency, I would argue, were those, like Ginsberg, Orlovsky, Corso, and DeLattre, who were more concerned with the ways in which the world had defeated others than with their own defeats. Despite the beat insistence on disengagement and individuality, the more introspectively personal a poem was, the less beat it was. The beats sought indeed to move beyond resentment.

Chapter Four
Upbeat and Offbeat

The downbeat frequency is sounded in the opening line of *Howl,* but the upbeat originated in the "Footnote" to *Howl,* which Mark Schorer understood as saying "that in spite of all of the depravity that *Howl* has shown, all of the despair, all of the defeat, life is essentially holy and should be so lived."[1] Such a perception of the sacrality of all things requires, as Ginsberg explained at the 1982 celebration of the twenty-fifth anniversary of the publication of *On the Road,* "a declaration of *unworldly love* that has *no hope* of the world and cannot change the world to its desire . . . [and is] totally open."[2] One cannot see the world in terms of one's own personally distorted desires, nor as one has been told, taught, forced, or conned into seeing it; one must view the world as one experiences it. One cannot hope to coerce the world into conformity with one's limited understanding; one must try to expand one's understanding to fit the world one finds. Above all, one cannot *tell* others what to do. One can lead those who need help, but we must all discover the world for ourselves if both the holiness of the individual and the world are to remain inviolate.

The downbeat poets called attention to the violations that the world has suffered as a result of individual ignorance or collective mischief and sought to shock the reader's consciousness into wakefulness. The upbeat poets celebrated the sacrality of the world and aspired to call but not coerce others to recognize it.

As we have seen, the first third of the *Beatitude Anthology* is dominated by the downbeat—perhaps only a modest amount of pessimism in proportion to the contemporary state of the world. The first and only break comes almost a quarter of the way through the collection: after the discomforting contributions of Orlovsky, Ginsberg, and Kerouac the next voice we hear is that of the senior reader that night in October 1955 at the Six Gallery.

Philip Whalen

Philip Whalen is a native of the American Northwest who has become a Buddhist monk. If this book were to have a hero, he would be it; but this is not a book about heroes, it is a book about beats. Whalen has always been diffident about being called a beat. One can understand why. "Beats" and "beatniks," as we have observed, have become confused, and Whalen is certainly no beatnik. Even the term "beat" has become associated with certain things—a quest for sensation, excitement, publicity, and the exotic, promiscuous behavior—that he rejects. Yet he comes as close to being a model figure of the purest aspirations of the beats as one could find.

Certainly he contributed the keynote to the *Beatitude Anthology* with his frequently reprinted poem, "In Which I Renounce the Notion of All Social Responsibility," a meditation on one of the most controversial aspects of the beat point of view, which Whalen has apparently had considerable trouble clarifying. The poem is difficult to empathize with because after initially setting forth the problem, he cloaks his response in a metaphor that, like most of his metaphors, is uncompromisingly personal and often obscure in its allusions.

"The minute I'm out of town," his friends encounter problems and write him worrying letters. "Am I their brains, their better sense?" he asks. "All of us want something to do," he continues, "but we must give our friends "a crack at being bodhisattvas [a buddhist term for those who have become enlightened] / (although their benevolence is a heavy weight on my head / their good intentions an act of aggression)" (30). The speaker apparently is having the all too frequent human urge to tell people what to do, how to straighten out their lives, but he feels it is really in their best interest to resist that urge. Certainly this interpretation of the poem is reinforced by Whalen's later statement that he enjoys teaching but "I cannot and will not solve any problems or answer any questions."[3] He apparently conceives of teaching in the Platonic sense of leading others to find their own answers instead of indoctrinating them or setting down rules. (After thirty years Hollywood has finally gotten around to producing what can be called a true San Francisco Poetry Renaissance film: Australian director Peter Weir's *Dead Poets Society* (1989)—set in the Beat year of 1959—dramatizes the conflict between a Whalen-like teacher, portrayed by Robin Williams, and his Chicago cop–like superiors.)

In "I Renounce . . ." Whalen is presenting a cardinal principle of the upbeat sensibility (also exemplified in Williams's role in Weir's film, though he is not called a beat)—that one must encourage others to fulfill themselves rather than use them for one's self-aggrandizement. This is also what Whitman urges in "Song of Myself" when he leads "each man and each woman of you" upon a knoll to point out "landscapes of continents and the public road. . . . Not I, not any one else can travel that road for you, / You must travel it for yourself" (section 46).[4]

The "beat road" was thus "the perpetual journey" of the American transcendentalists. This is not to say that Whalen has managed to maintain an invariably upbeat posture any more than Thoreau or Whitman could. Even the most self-effacing guide becomes at times exasperated, as Whalen does when he breaks out with "There's probably *Some* sensible human way of living in America / Without being rich or drunk or taking dope all the time."[5] Nor is he fatuously hopeful: "We complain of Tiberius in the White House / But consider: Caligula / Waits fretfully in some provincial capital." (Is this a reference to Sacramento?)[6]

As his statement in Donald Allen's anthology illustrates, however, Whalen shares the views of Thoreau and Whitman about nature and a simplified life: "My life has been spent in the midst of heroic landscapes which never overwhelmed me and yet I live in a single room in the city."[7] Whalen's work has never received anything like the consideration that it merits because he has steadfastly refused (like other beats who have less to offer) to compromise with audiences in order to find a ready market. Asked if he felt that not having money had affected his life and writing, he replied, "No, it's just inconvenient not to have any and then sometimes it's a drag not having any because there's nothing to eat and I like to eat, and . . . it's embarrassing to have to go about at that point to see people, to have to borrow money, or say, 'Invite me to dinner please because there isn't any food.'. . . it's so time consuming." When the persistent interviewers asked what he would want to do if he had money, he continued, "Well, what I know I'd do would simply be to read and write and play music and walk around as usual, that's all, the thing is, I wouldn't have to be worrying about where to find the bread."[8]

The Nature Lovers

Thoreauvean echoes are heard frequently in upbeat poetry and are more joyously expressed in Barbara Moraff's "Pome" than in Whalen's work. If any beat writing is to be anthologized it should certainly be "Pome," for it exactly captures the exuberant upbeat most critics have overlooked. It begins with the speaker "sitting nude & naked on an old tree- / stump rooted to silence . . . as the voice of orion this universe sprawled memory wide / beneath us." After musing over her few treasures and speculating that "maybe god is an unemployed comedian," she ends up "content to sit here on this treestump / gunung api [*sic*] flicking my cigareet so you may have stars" (83–84). Stars rather than advice is what she has to offer, certainly a more inspiring gift. The picture is of someone in perfect harmony with nature.

Nothing else by Barbara Moraff appears in the available issues of *Beatitude*, but she is one of the few beat writers who appeared in *Evergreen Review* after its first excited response to the San Francisco scene. "Tune" is a song for "lots of fresh girl-bodies," and "This Poem Has No Title" is a cryptic account of Chon K'on Tien, who kept a wife for each season in the same cave, where "they dont get along."[9] Her poems also appeared in the prestigious *Carleton Miscellany* and in *The Outsider.*

Her name disappeared from magazines after 1963, but Diane Di Prima mentioned in a 1978 interview that Moraff was a potter in Vermont and was still writing.[10] Shortly afterwards Moraff began to produce a series of chapbooks that appeared throughout the 1980s—*Deadly Nightshade* (1982), *Learning to Move* (1982), *Potterwoman* (1983), *Telephone Company Repairman Poems (1983), and Contra la Violencia* (1985), for example—from such offbeat sources as Toothpaste Press and Potes and Poets. After two decades an almost forgotten beat voice was being heard again.

The pastoral charm of Moraff's "Pome" pervades the work of William J. Margolis, who made what may be called the most affirmative contribution to the *Beatitude Anthology.* Margolis was one of the most prolific poets associated with the poetry renaissance, and it was an issue of his Berkeley poetry journal, *The Miscellaneous Man,* that was also involved at first in the obscenity case against *Howl.* He had begun the journal in April 1954; he identified the figure in his title as "the human being who, as a dynamic entity, never quite fits under any label and is constantly bulging out of categories. He stands alone, but not aloof; self-sufficient, and yet co-operative. . . . He is seeking and testing creative approaches to the problems that face individual men and women, that limit their humanity and chain them in a cage of mere existence."[11] Contributors to the first issue included Lawrence Lipton and other members of the Los Angeles group of innovative poets, Judson Crews and Mason Jordan Mason, and Lilith Lorraine, a dynamic figure who delivered two avant-garde poetry magazines, *Different* and *Flame,* from the remote west Texas community of Alpine and directed Avalon International, a worldwide association of poets for fostering a unified world culture. Lorraine contributed a vicious denunciation of suburban commuters, and Margolis himself provided a short story about a pacifist executed for treason who is regenerated to work for peace by something called "Transitional Phenomena," which had been suppressed by official scientists.

Three Margolis poems appear in the *Beatitude Anthology:* "Nexus," about a fascinating woman who "walked away" with the speaker's eyes; "Bites," which praises first another's hand and then each finger; and "Yes," which uses only nineteen words to make the point that though "we can't know who wound us up," we can know and thank those "who turned us on" (64–65)—certainly as upbeat a sentiment as one could look for. Neither Margolis nor Lilith Lorraine are recalled in Ann Charters's *The Beats*. While they are not earthshaking poets, they are as memorable as many who have been remembered, and they certainly did make prodigious efforts to shake up a world in which, as Lorraine puts it in "Daylight Saving," "television castrates thought."[12]

Closest to Margolis's attitude of affirmation is Richard Gumbiner, one of the demonstrators protesting police harassment of the beatniks in early 1960. An excerpt in the *Beatitude Anthology* from his *The Canticle of the Wanderer* qualifies him as the anthology's most enthusiastic adherent of the old euphoric Western concept of the frontier; he tells his "Beloved among the orchards"— ". . . we together shall defy / The wilderness, and in our time / Shall see the wilderness bear fruit" (87).

The upbeat women contributors, however, seemed less hopeful of escaping from the wilderness to realize the pioneers' dream of, as the old song goes, "a sweet little nest somewhere in the West." Anabel Kirby, a frequent contributor to *Beatitude* who was represented in the anthology by five selections, depicts in "Train of Thought" a prodigal son who hears a call to "Come back!" to his native pastures, though he "should have known / that's no use," and at last he does see that "he never would return" (77). But the road proves a perilous place, too; in "Poem," "The captive and captor strike out for themselves" but turn "to beckon a last / goodbye—too late" when they find "the sky empty—at the place where the road harkens" (76). In the strangest and most original of her poems, "Interior and Music," the author nevertheless presents a powerful case for the outdoor life as compared to an indoor life fueled by traditional art: "Classical music / dripping from the eaves, / Making a rainy day of it / Indoors / While the sun shines . . ." (78, ellipsis in text). But the writer, identified only as "Jo," finds no comfort outdoors at all, and in three poems deploring the long, cold night reaches the climax in her appeal, "Hold me darling / So close / there's not an inch between / us" (72).

Another nature lover was also quite skeptical about the prospects of making the wilderness bloom. Although A. (Alice) Pankovits, another frequent contributor to early issues of *Beatitude,* expressed in "Progress" "the wish to go down to the sea again," she switched the usual perspective by making the primitivistic viewpoint the upbeat one (as Kurt Vonnegut would do in

Galapagos during his postapocalyptic years). She took a position diametrically opposed to Richard Gumbiner's by stridently beginning, "I am not only going to stand in the way of progress / I am going to stick out my foot as it runs past." She scoffs at those who fancy they have conquered the elements and, in an early show of ecological concern, depicts the laughing sea, tossing back against "her shores and shoals derisively—beer cans, orange peels, waxed paper, soggy lettuce, pop bottles, paper bags, cigarette butts." This speaker desires to go "Back to nature . . . The pure, unsullied beauty" (85). It may take a beachcomber's sensibility to find this the most rousing poem in the book.

Nature does not always provide, however, the solace that Pankovits sought in it. Leo Younger in an untitled poem reflected the old romantic preoccupation with mutability in his lament that "the intensity / of things that are . . . disturb no suns, move no star" (102). Probably even closer to the upbeat frequency are some early poems by another writer who would become one of California's most prolific in more activist times, George Hitchcock, known principally for his discerning judgment in finding new voices for his journal *Kayak* (1964–84). His "Matin" suggests the inability of nature alone to overcome the fatal attraction of a civilized greed for money. Finding one morning a stockbroker lying dead among "the usual birdsongs," the speaker doubts the broker died from "natural causes," as "they say," and he takes to "drinking wine" (100).

Toward Beatnik Poetry

Even such a hedonistic retreat, harking back to Omar Khayyám, is rejected by the speaker in David Meltzer's "18th. Raga / Fall." Meltzer is a prolific poet best known for his *The San Francisco Poets* (1971), a collection of interviews with prominent beats at the time their fortunes were at low ebb. He was born in New York in 1937, the son of professional musicians, and as a child he sang regularly on radio's "Horn and Hardart's Children's Hour," the once famed automats' Sunday show that helped many talented children launch their careers. He found his vocation when in 1957, twenty, he moved to San Francisco and became a friend of Michael McClure, Lew Welch, and John Wieners. His claim to being a "second generation Beat writer" only serves, however, to rouse suspicions about all such claims, for rather than moving the frontiers of poetry he has concentrated on raising his large family.[13]

Meltzer's contributions to the *Beatitude Anthology* tend to retreat into nostalgia. Although his verse, like Pankovits's, has a downbeat flavor in its tendency to look backward, it leaves an upbeat aftertaste because of the mellowness his speakers find in lost dream worlds. In "18th. Raga / Fall" the speaker recalls that when he was thirteen and attracted to a sixteen-year-old Italian girl posing "in a tilted doorway" in coldly named Rockville Center on a street that "held / more fall sorrow than / . . . 10 million surrealist poems," he found that she was not looking back at him; he could only go home and see "her face in a hothouse sequence / kiss my loins & steam my ears" (41–42). In "Prayerwheel / 2—for John Wieners," he finds a metaphor for "the dissolution of love" in "the gone Bond sign—once high / above Broadway." (He is referring to an animated sign for a ready-to-wear clothing firm that stretched a whole city block over New York's Times Square in the early 1950s.) But, he asks, "Is anything ever gone / to the poet who works up everything / eventually?" (42–43).

Such passivity dissolves in Christopher MacLaine's "Break the Cake" into the frantic neurosis of one "who could never work in a room alone." The bemused third-person narrator is unusual in this collection which consists largely of first-person confessions. The character depicted is definitely downbeat and finally paralyzed by indecisiveness. The poem ends with a little note he writes himself: "Write suicide note moment you / walk through door / Tear up suicide note / Commit suicide / First go over, talk to redhead" (45). The observer, however, is nonchalantly upbeat about such histrionics.

Toward Consciousness of Tradition: Another Stock Report

Another upbeat tendency manifests itself toward the end of the anthology—in the work of those who had moved away from the beat frequencies by turning not to activism but to art for art's sake in revivals of traditional poetic forms. In view of the frequent dismissals of beat poetry as formless as well as aimless, it is surprising to find in the anthology several impressive efforts to meet the challenge of elaborate verse forms.

The last three pages of verse are devoted to haiku, six of them by John Chance—who departed from the strict seventeen-syllable Japanese form—and five of them, in the traditional form, by Daniel J. Langton, the poet who Robert Stock, in his 1957 letter dismissing the renaissance, singled out as one of the few worthy of attention in San Francisco and as one who was distinctly not a beat.

Chance's haiku are impressionistic images that mix downbeat and upbeat images of fright and pleasure. Langton used the three-line form not only to compress a terse statement into each haiku but also to create a culminating progression of images of day and night, death and life, that move from a call for spring during dark winter to a promise of the new season's arrival. Langton is indeed a skillful and sensitive artist, and there is little beat disengagement in his thoughtful concern for blending style and substance in a traditional cycle of the seasons. Giving him almost the last word in the anthology indicates a respect for traditional art not on the beat frequency—perhaps an instance of Ferlinghetti's taste prevailing over the beat sensibility.

The very last word is reserved, however, for a haiku that disregards traditional rules. Lew Gardner's statement in fourteen syllables appropriately ends the anthology by summing up the way the beats must have seen themselves and their relation to the surrounding culture, which, Thomas Parkinson pointed out, they had changed "through the creation—or recognition—of a new audience" (285):

> The silent pool
> Is rippled now
> The center is in us. (107)

Before the end, however, Robert Stock himself has turned up; somewhat surprisingly, his rupture with the beats was apparently patched up.[14] He contributed two poems in quite artificial and highly demanding forms. A villanelle, "Paul Klee," celebrates in a distinctly upbeat voice how "beyond tamed Europe" the whimsical Swiss artist, "like a child . . . hazards wisdom where beginnings are," "beguiled" by such relics of the past as "runic stone or skeleton" (98). The tone changes in "Pantoum on Some Lines from Camoens"; this by-product of the poet's long engagement in translating Portugal's epic bard equivocally asks questions and provides no answers, no reasons for "so much burdening necessity!" (*Tanta necessidade aborrecida!*) (99).

Perhaps even more surprising is the use of a traditional sonnet form in one of the most upbeat statements in the volume. John Richardson, the only identifiably black poet in the book besides Bob Kaufman, dedicated "Rosa Mundi" to Gilbert Sorrentino (prominently associated with the East Coast beats).[15] He pays tribute to the beauty of "the Rose of This World (daily efflorescent)" but praises even more highly its "sempiternal" recurrence in "the beauty that [man] knows / to have been and to be: the poet's rose" (97).

Among the traditionally inspired poems, just before the haiku, is another work with an Oriental flavor that deserves special attention. Although it is simply an imagistic rendition of the shimmering "dragonfly" of its title, the poem, by David Rafael Wang, one of the most interesting contributors to the anthology, is the only one of Oriental origin.

David Rafael Wang

David Hsin-fu Wand (the name he first used in America) was born in Hangchow, China, under the sign of Capricorn, during the winter of 1931–32. He was a direct descendant of a major Tang dynasty (701–61) painter and poet, whose works he translated. He left his homeland in 1949 at the time when Mao Tse-tung defeated Chiang Kai-shek's national forces. Wand entered Dartmouth College and anglicized his name to David Rafael Wang, with which he signed most of his poems. He acclimated himself quickly and served as class poet for the class of 1955.

His first book, a sixteen-page, hand-printed pamphlet, *The Goblet Moon,* bears no publisher's name or date but is apparently the collection that won him an undergraduate poetry prize at Dartmouth in 1954.[16] It is of extraordinary interest because the contents appear to have been placed in chronological order of composition and thus the pamphlet provides a unique record of the transformation of a sensitive and talented writer, trained in an Oriental tradition, into a substantial contributor to beat poetry. The collection begins with three translations from Chinese; no authors are identified, but the poems sound much like his own work written at Dartmouth. The second begins:

> Spotting the moonlight at my bedside,
> I wonder if it is frost on the ground.
> After raising my head to look at the bright moon
> I lower it to think of the old country.

This tranquil image is followed by more agitated verses in English, including a skiing poem, "Slalom," that shares the New England imagery of Robert Frost's "Birches." Another poem, "Bas-Relief," is marked by a transition from Oriental politeness to Western frankness, suggesting Wang's first affinities with the emerging beats, of whom he had probably not yet heard. In a conversation, the change of tones and play on words suggest that the speakers may be the poet's old and new selves:

> "Life, copulation, and death are disgusting," quoth he,
>   "The only relief is art."
> "But what is art," say I, "but a relief of life,
>   copulation and death?"

On the next page, he reverts to Oriental imagery: a "little junk" drifting slowly into a creek, a derelict walking in the woods and startling wild ducks, and finally, "Vespers," which seems almost a parody of Chinese clichés:

> In the depth of a bamboo forest
> I hear the chime of the temple bells;
> Watching twilight upon the lotus petals,
> I linger about the mountains' edge.

"Vespers" could well have been intended as a farewell to the formal poetic language an imagery of his past: the next poem is not only entitled "Awakening" but comes as a shock after the decorousness of the previous poems, with its imitation of Dylan Thomas (who fascinated many aspiring young poets during his American tours before his death in 1953):

> When I was young and lazy as the snow
> And loved to roll and loll upon the shore
> Of a splendid vision, silken into air
> Soaring phoenix-like across my wind-swept brain
> I chose no friends among the mocking herd
> But bridged my thought toward the mighty dead. . . .

A tone more rebellious against the past than inspired by it infuses the next poem, dedicated to a friend. The speaker protests that he does not want to be the dragon, phoenix, or unicorn of mythology, "I don't want to be different / I want to be just like you." This note of protest intensifies in what might be called—in its foreshadowing of some tendencies Wang later discussed in his work—an antiliterary poem, "The Alexandrian Flame," which urges that

> books be burnt—
> like incense to the ghosts,
> Who strike no chord except Platonic love,
> Who touch no music vibrant in the spring
> Of mystic wombs and potent phalluses.

The Goblet Moon ends with a sonnet that concludes:

> When once it was my fashion to write a play
> To present on the stage of your mind,
> I decided to go raving mad and blind.

Wang thus was beginning to suppress intellectuality in favor of hedonistic sensation at the same time that the beats were circulating underground the works that many would look at askance for fostering such attitudes. Wang supported the beat view in the introduction to his second book of poems, *The Intercourse;* he stated that "the overemphasis on the intellect in American universities tends to stifle the imagination."[17] There he listed among his models Robert Creeley and Denise Levertov.

After graduating he worked with William Carlos Williams while obtaining a master's degree in creative writing through the program at San Francisco State College. In view of his changing sensibility, it is not surprising that during this period he began collaborating with Philip Whalen and Gary Snyder, who were as interested in Oriental traditions as he was in American practices. He also became a frequent contributor to *Beatitude,* where he published in August 1959 a letter to Ezra Pound that was quite at variance with the serenity of his poem "Dragonfly."

Although he was almost fifty years younger than Pound Wang had hoped to study with the older poet, "to pay respects to one who served Chinese culture;" but he dropped this plan on discovering that Pound "abandon[ed] Confucius, whom he pretended to serve." Almost a year later, in June 1960, Wang published in *Beatitude* 15 the even more surprising "Proclamation: from a sick bourgeois," which attacks Mao Tse-tung. Wang says, "I would like to spit on your melon face, to dismiss you as a nuisance," but finds that he "cannot even bring myself to burn you in effigy" because "you size up the world with a single line of a poem."

While working for the *Chinese World* in San Francisco, Wang was also finding other outlets for his poems. In the same issue of *Poetry Broadside* in which Robert Stock attacked Ginsberg and Corso, a two-page spread was devoted to a long feature on four cantos of Wang's "Grandfather Cycle." In his introduction, he commented on his indebtedness to Pound, as well as Chaucer, Shakespeare, and Blake, and explained that in this poetic "appreciation of the achievement of my noble forebears" he would "like to use the English language to approximate Chinese speech."[18] The selections from the work in progress superficially resemble the form of Pound's *Cantos,* but they lack the juxtapositions of allusions that have kept the Pound explicators busy while turning off the less cabalistically inclined. Wang's four cantos move from an astonishing account of "the epic fornications of my fabulous Grandfather" to the description of a mansion that made even the Empress jealous, then to an account of his grandfather's scholarly achievements, which led to the Emperor's sending him to France, Belgium, Luxembourg, and Germany, until his grandfather insisted on retiring in order to spend his remaining years with his numerous progeny.

Even this chronicling of his grandfather's activities in public and private could scarcely prepare readers for the course that Wang's poetry was to follow after his long disappearance from the beat magazines where he had frequently published. To provide one answer to the question of what became of old beats, Wang, like a number of others, spent his time in the 1960s acquiring a doctorate in comparative literature from the University of Southern California. He attained a respectable academic position at the State University of New York College at Geneseo and, using the name David Happell Hsin-Fu Wand, wrote *The Use of Native Imagery by Chinese Poets Writing in English* (1973) and *Asian-American Heritage* (1974), an anthology of contemporary Oriental writings neglected, he thought, because of "whites' indifference or discrimination against ethnic mixture."[19]

He had not forsaken his earlier aspirations, however, and his next publication marked a return to poetry; *The Intercourse* was indeed about the sexual variety. It is divided into three sections, "The Thrust," "The Insertion," and "The Withdrawal." Wand had remarked in *Asian-American Heritage* that he had been found by most of his friends "to be rather anti-intellectual in my poetry" and indeed his turn to explicit sexual material mirrored the direction taken in the later works of Michael McClure and Lenore Kandel.

The "thrust" of the first section title is adequately suggested by the description in "Intaglio" of "his hardness waking / in the caress of her hand"[13]; The second section "The Insertion," deals quite graphically with what many readers would probably regard as deviant practices, as in the narrator's description in the title poem of his bedding down with his wife and another man:

> the filthy
> thought of all three of us
> .in the same bed
> making it
> would churn the
> stomach of our puritan fathers of
> which—thank god—I have none to boast. (28)

Homoerotic references—present also especially in the Samoan sections of *Asian-American Heritage,* persist in "The Withdrawal": the narrator's partner is compared to Apollo, until

> when you open
> your mouth
> your nimbus
> fades and you are
> but another ranch-
> hand washing his face. (36)

Wang also commented in *The Intercourse* that he was continuing work on "the Grandfather Cycle" and that part of it would shortly appear in *Rivers of Fire.* But this volume appears not to have been published before Wang's early death on 8 April 1977, ironically, just at the time that the summer writing programs at Naropa Institute in Boulder, to which he might have made a unique contribution, were beginning to stimulate new interests in the beats. His career offers, however, an upbeat study not only of the assimilation of an artist from another culture into the American avant-garde but also of the role of the poetry renaissance in such a transformation.

Offbeat

Several contributors to the *Beatitude Anthology,* including some of the best known, were communicating on a frequency distinctly different from the beats frequency, as we have seen from the haiku of Daniel Langton. The most conspicuous of these was Lawrence Ferlinghetti, who selected the contents for the volume. Despite Ferlinghetti's unparalleled efforts to promote the beats, he has resisted, justifiably, the application of the label to himself. Several differences between his aims and theirs have already been pointed out, and his position is certainly made clear by his own two pieces in the anthology, as well as by his many other writings. Significantly, he did not place his own works up front with the principal beats—Ginsberg, Kerouac, Corso, Whalen, McClure—but well back in the volume with Bob Kaufman and William Margolis, both of whom tended to be more socially committed and activist-minded than the beats saw any reason to be in a generally hopeless world where the principal concern needed to be individual integrity.

We have already seen how the beginning of Ferlinghetti's "Loud Prayer" provides an appropriate afternote to Bob Kaufman's satirical note, and perhaps its ending—"deliver us from evil / whose presence remains unexplained / in thy kingdom of power and glory / oh man"—is an appropriate expression here of the concept the beats rejected: that there may be superior powers exercising some control over human destiny. This idea surfaces even in the midst of a passage about a search for sexual ecstasy in his prose work *Her:* with a bit of the malicious playfulness found often in his work, he says, "I'll be off to see . . . the wonderful wizard of *odds against me* in the nowhere void" (63, emphasis added). In Ferlinghetti's concern for getting poetry back in the streets where it belongs there is still something of the revolutionary attitude of "manning the barricades" that the beats distrusted.

A more surprising contributor to *Beatitude* is the only young writer just making a start who would subsequently flourish briefly as one of the writers most admired by the hippies, who took over San Francisco from the beats. Richard Brautigan had moved to the city from the state of Washington in 1954, when he was nineteen and the beats were just gathering. He quickly became associated with them and lived for a time with Philip Whalen. In 1955, he was included in the book *Four New Poets* from a local press; the others—Martin Hoberman, Carl Larsen, and James M. Singer—were not affiliated with the beats. Brautigan remained generally underground, as Kerouac had earlier, during the San Francisco Poetry Renaissance and did not emerge—to become what may best be called the post-beat idol of the hippies—until 1967, when *Trout Fishing in America* was published.[20]

As that book suggests, one of the things that most conspicuously distinguished Brautigan and the post-beat sensibility—manifested most outrageously by Ken Kesey's Merry Pranksters—was whimsical and fantastic humor. As already noted in the discussion of Bob Kaufman, humor was not the beats' strong point; upbeat or downbeat, they did not find the world's situation absurdly funny. The beats were too intense and the beatniks too languorous to pump out catchy one-liners; they did not cultivate the offhand manner of stand-up comedians. Even the beats' visionary works, even Kerouac's dreams, always express a deep sympathy for unspoiled nature, a sense of connectedness with real places they hold in high esteem, and an overweening anger that this reality is being threatened that allows no time for escapist fun and games. In the succeeding psychedelic era, dreams overwhelmed an experiential sense of the world.

Brautigan's detachment was observable from his earliest publications; "Kingdom Come" published in *Epos* (1958), presents twilight as "a place of spells and visions"—like the vision of an old woman who appears to be crying but then stops a taxi and gets in with a plum tree she is carrying, and that's it. His pieces in *Beatitude Anthology* display this same, ultimately pointless, whimsy. The American submarine of the poem of that title is Edgar Allan Poe sailing beneath a herd of Nebraska buffaloes who do not hear a sound. But his most deliriously imaginative contribution is "The Whorehouse at the Top of Mount Rainier," which describes the French poet Baudelaire's visit to this imaginary institution under the impression that "there would be / Eskimo women." When he discovers his mistake, "Baudelaire shit / his pants" (36).

The beats evidently enjoyed this kind of whimsy (particularly if they were high enough), although they did not produce it themselves, and the vulgarity of the Baudelaire poem also certainly appealed to their desire to shock the bourgeois. But there is a superficiality in Brautigan—like that of an impish little boy outraging his prim elders—that makes it ludicrous to try to associate his work with anything like the despair of Jonathan Swift's "excremental vision."

Brautigan's contributions are followed by two Stan Persky poems that also deal with nineteenth-century French poets and also deviate widely from characteristic beat postures. Persky is of particular interest because he is— except for Ginsberg and Orlovsky—the only one who was subsequently represented in anthologies of gay poetry. The prominence and flamboyance of Ginsberg and Orlovsky have created the impression that if not all the beats were gay, at least a substantial number were homosexuals who exercised a disproportionate influence upon beat sensibility. But this impression is a mistake; although the beats tended to be tolerant and were rarely homophobic, there was little gay propaganda in *Beatitude*. The gays did not arrive in force in San Francisco until the Castro Street days following gay liberation in 1969–70, and Persky did not remain associated with the beats for very long. His contributions to the anthology are puzzlingly ambiguous. In "The Beautiful Head of Rimbaud," the masochistic speaker who protests, "I who in this world love women," expresses nevertheless an infatuation for "Rimbaud of infinite beauty," for whom he would remove his "gloves" "in this hotel room / of Tombstone Arizona 1860's." The speaker ends by asking to be blessed quickly for having "sinned excessively" (37– 38). "Apollinaire," arranged as a prose poem, is neither gay nor beat, and the presence of this surrealist collage is the most difficult to understand. It opens with Apollinaire, whose teeth are falling out, visiting a dentist's office at the same time as Gertrude Stein and moves then to his mother at home cooking spaghetti. The only indication of the narrator's interest in these celebrities is the final line: "It is nice to leave Apollinaire in Italy—naked— morning—with cold feet—his prime" (39). No telling why, except that Persky liked to write about naked men.

The final offbeat contribution, and the only one by a woman, is another surrealist piece—"Dracula" by Francine Marshall, who has no other ascertainable connection with the poetry renaissance. Even more than Brautigan's bagatelles, this poem is an ephemeral one-liner about Dracula's first visitor in ten years. When the visitor, who is not described at all, observes that the vampire must be lonesome, he replies, "I have diversions / . . . So glad to see you" (86).

Perhaps the poems grouped here are not the ones referred to in the introduction to *Beatitude Anthology* as not on "the beat frequency" but just examples of the beat taste in humor. If so, the humor is grotesque and morbid, and it is not surprising that little has been said about it. The beats were certainly not temperamentally inclined to turn out the mindless nonsense of American situation comedies, which are designed to help audiences escape reality rather than confront it.

Chapter Five
Pacific Outposts

Since over the years the Beat Generation has become exclusively identified with San Francisco, anyone who chanced today on a book that proclaimed itself "the first complete inside story" of that generation would be quite nonplussed to find the beats situated not in the coffeehouse of North Beach but in a rundown seaside suburb of Los Angeles. So diffident were the beats about the possibility of their possessing lasting historical significance that it apparently never occurred to anyone on the San Francisco scene to prepare any kind of "guidebook," perhaps in the manner of John Gunther's popular "inside" stories of various earthshaking locales. At least, none were issued at the time or have subsequently surfaced.[1]

The book touted by the advertisement quoted above was *The Holy Barbarians* (1959) by Lawrence Lipton, the oldest individual to attach himself to beat coattails when they appeared to offer the road to some quick bucks. The book's setting is Venice West, which was best introduced by Lipton himself in his opening chapter as "Slum by the Sea."

Venice West

"This is Venice by the Pacific," Lipton began, "dreamed up by a man named Kinney at the turn of the century, a nineteenth-century man of vision, a vision as trite as a penny postal card. He went broke in heart and pocket trying to carry his Cook's Tour memories of the historic city on the Adriatic into the twentieth century. . . . All that remains of Kinney's Folly are a few green-scum-covered canals."[2] Lipton used this decaying souvenir of *la belle epoque* as his setting because he lived there and because "it has afforded me an opportunity to watch the formation of a community of disaffiliates from its inception."

Actually, Lipton's slum was by no means a plantation for beat emigrants from the foggy Bay Area to sunny southern California. Here grew an indigenous enclave trying to produce not a renaissance but a first flowering of the arts in a region where only recently, as one of its historians put it, the cattle had roamed on a thousand hills. Such efforts had been going on for some time in the environs of Los Angeles, which was lousy with money from the

87

flourishing film industry but lacked the éclat of the unimpressed older city up the coast. We have already observed in Chapter 2 the annoyance of some locals at Louis Simpson's provincial Eastern ignorance of the existence in Los Angeles of an arts community attempting, without conspicuous success, to rival the beats who were receiving an increasingly irritating amount of publicity.[3]

A number of literary journals were launched in the area during the period between 1955 and 1960. The most notable was the slick and eye-catching *Coastlines,* edited by Mel Weisburd in Hollywood, with Bard Dahl as fiction editor and Gene Frumkin as poetry editor. It survived for twenty-two issues over almost ten years (1955–64). Los Angelenos could always come up with the money to package their inferior product more glossily than the usually out-of-pocket San Franciscans; but none of their efforts attracted much more than local interest.

When the *Howl* trial began to focus national attention on California, the Los Angeles contingent began to associate themselves with the North Beach set, especially when the always footloose beats dropped in for some sun and bread. The Autumn 1957 issue of *Coastlines* reprinted an excerpt from William Hogan's "A Few Cool Words for *Howl*" from his "Between the Lines" column in the *San Francisco Chronicle,* where he was book editor. Hogan called *Howl* "the most significant single long poem to be published in this country since World War II, perhaps since Eliot's *Four Quartets.*" He described the poem as "a *gestalt,* an archetypal configuration of the mass culture which produced it," and also as "a condemnation of our official culture." He argued that perhaps the collector of customs deserved a medal for doing in a day what "it would have taken years for critics to accomplish"— making the poem famous.[4]

A note a few pages further on informed readers of Lawrence Lipton's formation of "a lively group of experimental poets," headquartered at the Venice West Poetry Center on Ocean Front Walk. The group included Stuart Perkoff, Charles Newman, Charles Foster, Saul White, and Bruce Boyd. (Perkoff {1930–74} rated an entry in Ann Charter's *The Beats,* but the others were unremembered.) The group had played host on 2 August to Jonathan Williams, the energetic poet, publisher, and promoter from North Carolina, and had read poems by Rexroth, Ferlinghetti, and Ginsberg at recent poetry and jazz sessions.

In the next issue, Lipton, described as a previous contributor, was represented by what was probably in its day the best-known poem from the Venice West group, "I Was a Poet for the FBI." The speaker describes himself as "Poet in Residence at *Time, Life,* and *Fortune,* who found an atheist in a foxhole and reported him to MacArthur." He was also "Ed Hoover's man at YMCA College collecting free verse in the ladies' room and once, disguised as Oscar Wilde, in the men's toilet."[5]

Although many of its allusions are now dated, the poem's verve and timeliness are somewhat surprising, since Lipton was almost sixty when it appeared, a member of Henry Miller's generation and much older than the well-known beats. He had been born in Lodz, Poland, in 1898 and brought to the United States by his father in 1903. Lipton came quite late to poetry; he had begun writing as a journalist in the 1920s. With his third wife, he coauthored twenty-two mystery novels in the 1930s and 1940s under the pen name of Craig Rice. He also wrote two serious protest novels, *Brother, The Laugh Is Bitter* and *In Secret Battle,* during World War II. His first volume of poetry did not appear until after he had been strongly influenced by Dylan Thomas in 1955; that book became a selection of the California Poetry Book Club.

By far his most successful undertaking; however, was *The Holy Barbarians.* By the time Lipton got around to it, there had been the same kind of break between the Venice West Poetry Center and the Hollywood group supporting *Coastlines* as had occurred between the beats and Rexroth and his cortege in San Francisco. Signs of strain were already showing when *Coastlines* published "I Was a Poet for the FBI"; its "Blunderbuss" column (on "what's going on up and down the coast") reported that the beats had dispersed and it reprinted Rexroth's derogatory comments from the December 1957 issue of *Frontier* about the beats being "a craze." The column also noted the full-scale attack on the beats in *Mainstream* (a journal published in Palatine, Illinois, unrelated to the Communist party's *Masses and Mainstream*) as a "plausible antidote to the San Francisco issue of *Evergreen Review.*" The unidentified "Blunderbuss" commentator did think the criticism was deserved, but thought *Mainstream* "doth protest too much."[6] Gene Frumkin also quoted "Squeal," Louis Simpson's parody of *Howl,* though he chided Simpson for not knowing about the existence of the Los Angeles avant-garde.[7]

Before Lipton published *The Holy Barbarians* in February 1959, a complete rupture had occurred; Lipton wrote spitefully of a reading by Allen Ginsberg that *Coastlines* had offered to sponsor:

I knew they had no use for the sort of thing Ginsberg was writing or what we were doing in Venice West (in fact, much of their magazine is devoted to attacking it), but now that it looked like it might be attracting wide public attention they wanted to get into the act.

The reading was to be held in a big old-fashioned house that was occupied by two or three of the *Coastline* [sic] editors, living in a kind of Left Wing bohemian collective household, furnished . . . in atrociously bad taste, nothing like the imaginative and original decor of the beat generation pad, even the most poverty-stricken. (194)

This last comment presents readers, both then and now, with the problem of deciphering Lipton's intentions in the book. He seemed to be confusing superficial aspects of beatnik fashion with the poetry renaissance as a literary force—just as much as did the editors of *Life* and other popular magazines trying to sensationalize the beats.

Indeed, most of *The Holy Barbarians* seems to be about beatniks rather than beats. The first and most often quoted section of Lipton's guidebook is a series of "case studies" in which it is impossible to distinguish fact from invention. These concern emotionally troubled misfits to whom Lipton gave names like Angel Ben Davis, Itchy Gelden, and Rhonda Tower. (Lipman's widow later wrote that some of the people who recognized themselves as models for these figures took on the names that Lipton had given them, thus completing the confusion of fact and fiction.)[8] Moving in the second section to a discussion of the "disaffiliation" that provided the common bond between these "outsiders," he maintained that they were not against "material things as opposed to spiritual things." Their "voluntary self-alienation from the family cult, from Moneytheism and all its works and ways" was attributable to their having found the answer to "the New Prosperity" in "the New Poverty," which was "not to be confused with the poverty of indigence, intemperance, improvidence or failure" but was "an independent, voluntary poverty" (149–50).

What he described more closely resembles, however, the rebellion against a strictly materialistic, consumer-oriented culture by those "outsiders" (like Britain's Angry Young Men) who still cherish nostalgic hopes of returning to some better traditional order they imagine to have existed in the past, than beatistic "*unworldly* love that has *no hope* of the world and cannot change the world to its desire." Lipton was conjuring up a revived arts and crafts movement rather than a spiritual awakening. There certainly is nothing wrong with an arts and crafts movement; most of the genuinely livable environments that can be found today have developed from such efforts, which have in recent decades proved considerably more successful than the beats' exertions. But nothing is explained by confusing such laudable exercises of taste, patience, and industry with those epiphanic, visionary moments that may have provided their impetus—as the Fauvists, for example, opened the way to Raoul Dufy's achievement as the century's greatest designer and decorator.

Lipton's vision was entirely inspired by European "outsider" traditions, and he displayed no sensitivity to the Oriental influences on the work of those beats who have proved most enduring—Ginsberg, Snyder, Whalen, Kandel—nor to the American example of Thoreau, who, as another opportunist has observed disdainfully, "elevated disconnection into a national ideological value."[9] Lipton was actually doing just what he accused the *Coastlines* coterie of doing—trying to "get into the act" once it had attracted national attention.[10]

Nowhere are his faulty premises more apparent than in his effort to make traditional New Orleans jazz the basis of a ritualistic life he sought to impose upon the beats. He was more uncompromising in this crusade to promote the synergy of jazz and the Beat than Rexroth or Ferlinghetti had ever been. Basing his whole concept of a populist culture on a jazz that was classic by 1955, Lipton, like Rexroth, failed to perceive the reason the improvisatory art he exalted had not enjoyed financial success in what he denounced as "the musical supermarket sense of the jazz festivals" (207): jazz was an elitist art for connoisseurs and had never been, as French aficionados of "le jazz hot" had early recognized, the popular music of American mass audiences. Only a small group of connoisseurs relished the legendary jazz that had emanated from New Orleans's raffish Storytown at the beginning of the century before moving on during the 1920s to the speakeasies of Kansas City and Chicago.

When jazz was toned down into "swing," the popular music of the big-band era of the 1930s and 1940s, melodic traditions from the music hall and the operetta almost submerged the spontaneous sound that decorous audiences found vulgar. The improvisatory jazz of the "jam sessions" of the years around World War II attracted only small, intense audiences for the experimenters—like Dan Jaffe and Herb Six, whose attempts at "jazz opera" were part of Kansas City's effort to reinvigorate its local tradition.[11]

What Rexroth and Lipton hoped to do was attract young audiences to poetry readings with jazz accompaniments so as to widen the audience for verse that was more demanding than that found on greeting cards or in popular song lyrics. By 1955 America's popular music had degenerated into a nondescript mélange ranging from the jingly "Ballad of Davy Crockett" and the exotic slinkiness of "Whatever Lola Wants" to the kitschy, candy-box sentimentality of "Love Is a Many-Splendored Thing."[12] Those loosely associated with the beat impulse saw an opportunity to appeal to bored young people by expanding nationally the kind of jazz performances that were just being revived at New Orleans's Preservation Hall.

The very next year, however, spelled doom to such hopes: in 1956, out of the red clay hills around Tupelo, Mississippi, sprang Elvis Presley to become overnight the biggest popular music sensation of the decade. Elvis combined with his provocative gestures that scandalized decent folks the musical traditions of southern jazz blues and country and western music, which had been steadily building audiences through the Grand Old Opry on Nashville's high-powered radio station WSM, whose transmissions penetrated into the boondocks everywhere. When Elvis appeared on national television in 1956 and on the screen in *Love Me Tender,* young audiences, to the despair of such would-be tastemakers as Lipton and Rexroth, chose their own way out of the musical doldrums. By the time Elvis disappeared for awhile into the army, rock and roll, which he had paved the way for, was firmly established and would hold center stage through the remaining years of the Beat. In the early 1960s as the beats were dispersing, the Beatles made their appearance in the United States, and the rock era had begun.

Although one would be hard put to find any literary or spiritual aspects in Elvis's art, his emergence at the same time as the beats is scarcely surprising, for he did share—especially with Kerouac and Cassady—the same kind of energy that drove the beats and appalled respectable people, and the same kind of spontaneity in the way he lived. He certainly did take music, and poetry of a sort, back out into the street, where Ferlinghetti had thought it should go; but Elvis's style and substance were not quite what Ferlinghetti had fancied street poetry should be, nor did the beats approve the replacement of improvisational jazz by rock and roll.

Traditional jazz has enjoyed a considerable revival, especially in New Orleans, and even ragtime has had an affectionate revival; but they have not attracted mass audiences. Those who staked their hopes on a cultural future shaped by a wedding of poetry and jazz had to watch the crowds head for rock concerts and Opryland. Lipton's *The Holy Barbarians* remains a provocative—though somewhat long-winded—record of a culture that existed more in the minds of its proponents and detractors than on the streets that Ferlinghetti hoped would extend far beyond North Beach and Venice West. And it certainly does not live up to its promise to tell the "complete inside story of the Beat Generation."

Lipton published one more book during his lifetime, *The Erotic Revolution* (1965), as the hippies' flower power movement was gaining momentum. His call for the repeal of all laws regarding sexual activity might have been expected to appeal to this group, but it attracted little notice. By that time the young were just taking the law into their own hands, and Lipton's idealistic notion of genteel poverty put him even further out of touch with the hippies and their successors than he had been with the beats.

On the whole, Los Angeles, a vast amalgam of suburbs with no heart, showed as little understanding of the beats as most of the rest of the country. Paradoxically, its most important poet—whose rise to late-found eminence was abetted by the attention to the beats, although he was never directly affiliated with them—was, to the horror of the Hollywood and even probably the Venice West set, Charles Bukowski. The city played no role, however, in getting him off to a good start. While he published in a number of little magazines around the country in the late 1950s, he received his most substantial boosts from the post-beat *Epos* in Crescent City, Florida, and, on the West Coast, from the small Northern California coastal town of Eureka, famed for its Victorian mansions.

Eureka's *Hearse*

The San Francisco Poetry Renaissance found remarkably little support in its native state. Hardly any of the little magazines it inspired in the late 1950s and early 1960s appeared in California communities outside the Bay Area. But the dynamic exception, Eureka's *Hearse: A Vehicle Used to Convey the Dead,* made up for this inattention with its intensity. It was edited single-handedly by E. V. Griffith, who described it in the first issue in 1956 as ". . . carrying poetry, prose, artwork and incidental cadaver to the Great cemetery of the American Intellect. . . ." In the second issue he added to this statement, "an irreverent quarterly"—certainly a fitting description for what proved to be the apotheosis of the downbeat through another seven issues published by 1961.

Griffith received few contributions from the most newsworthy beats, who by 1958 had no lack of outlets. Although his fifth issue did open with Allen Ginsberg's self-confrontational "Over Kansas" (which, as previously discussed, also appeared in the *Beatitude Anthology*), Griffith usually published works only by those closely associated with the beats. The first issue contained an illustration by Ferlinghetti, who had originally planned to be an artist; poems by Judson Crews and Jonathan Williams; a homoerotic collage, "Extinct Bird," attributed to Mercy Pennis Hyman; the first of occasional excerpts from Dick Stud's "Autobiography"; and a contribution by Langston Hughes, the distinguished black poet whom the beats much admired.

Hughes also appeared in the third issue, along with Robert Creeley,

Mason Jordan Mason, and Stuart Perkoff. Charles Bukowski turned up in this issue; "Some Notes on Dr. Klarstein," who hates "you" and "everybody," established Bukowski's affinity for the downbeat. He would contribute six more poems to the magazine by 1961. Bukowski was also published in the short-lived *Gallows,* edited in Eureka by E. V. Griffith's young brother Jon T. in 1959, and in *Coffin,* a portfolio of poems and graphics by several hands that was another Griffith venture. The most important service to Bukowski, however, was Griffith's sponsorship of Bukowski's first chapbook, *Flower, Fist and Bestial Wail;* this work is undated, but Bukowski's bibliographer says it was published in November 1960.[13]

Griffith launched the chapbook series in 1959 with selections from the work of Mason Jordan Mason and Gil Orlovitz. He followed up with the collection *Eye Poems,* collages by Griffith himself and others, including someone supposedly named Farley Gay, described in the "Coroner's Report" on the inside back cover of *Hearse* 4 as "closely watched for his art work and other activities." This issue also contained contributions by Stuart Perkoff and David Rafael Wang, who became a steady supplier of short poems about male models and hustlers, including a youth with a "Grecian profile envied by the gods" who "For five measly bucks [will] show you how to hump . . . / For a ten-dollar bill [will] spend the night with you."[14] Contributors to *Hearse* 3 included Kenneth Rexroth and Richard Brautigan. The fifth issue elicited from Leroi Jones "The Last Roundup," which appears to be about a racist incident on a college campus in the South—foreshadowing Jones's subsequent militancy as Imamu Amiri Baraka—but ends on a distinctly beat note as the speaker being hustled to the dean asks, "Loving them all / so much / WHAT could I say / ? / I said / "GRACIOUS, BEAUREGARD / HOW YOU DO GO ON / (& wept)."[15] A long poem by regular contributor John Barkley Hart, "The Flight of Mr. Sun," similarly couples militancy—"WILLIAM FAULKNER BURNED A BARN WE SHALL BURN A SCHOOL"—with a concluding hope that "Mr. Sun" "MAY YET SHAKE THE PATTERN / FROM THE CORE OF A HORROR / AS YET UNENVISIONED."[16]

Hearse 7 offers an impressive list of contributors. Langston Hughes, Gil Orlovitz, and Charles Bukowski are back, joined by popular novelist David Cornel DeJong and Diane Di Prima. Di Prima's lilting conclusion that "When Jeannie sings / Bach listens" is in disorienting contrast to the atmosphere evoked by "Diary of Anatole Tarsh," the downbeat meditation of an American suburbanite beset by fears of his own inadequacies and the ominous demands of his insensitive family ("Underneath rotten with maggots . . . Covered with green slime"), who dreams of escaping to "Bandung / Or

Rangoon or Kabul or someplace remote / From the moldy rind of experience."[18] One of the most historically interesting poems in the run of *Hearse* is Bukowski's embarrassingly personal, "I Am Visited By An Editor And A Poet." There can be no doubt about the identity of the monologuist who is visited in his beercan-strewn room, where he is listening to Italian opera:

> J. B. May [the editor of *Trace*] and Wolf the Hedley are very immaculate,
>   clean fingernails, etc.;
> I apologized for the beer cans, my beard, and everything
>   on the floor
> and pretty soon everybody was yawning. . . .

When he walks over and looks "at the five magazines with my name on the cover," he wonders "if we are writing poetry or all huddling in / one big tent / clasping assholes."[19] One gets a sense of the tensions that disrupted the unremarkable Los Angeles scene.

Griffith revived *Hearse* for another eight issues between 1969 and 1977 with a support grant from the Coordinating Council of Literary Magazines, which was backed in turn by the National Endowment for the Arts. Some of the old contributors, led by Bukowski, reappeared, but this much more elaborate, forty-eight-page journal had much of the museum quality of the Renaissance woodcuts that supplanted Farley Gay's "eye poems."

What had happened over the decade that the magazine lapsed is suggested by the title of Bukowski's "On Getting Famous and Being Asked: Can You Recite? Can You Be There at Nine?" and by the poem's complaining tone. There is a great deal of complaining in all the selections, but little vision. The Beat had given up residence in California even before the last of the old *Hearses* had carried its last cadavers, and resurrecting the old title did not bring the body back to life.[20]

Chapter Six
The Beat Goes On

The San Francisco Poetry Renaissance has not ended and never will as long as there remain a dedicated few plugging away to keep the beat frequencies operative. Most beats accepted exile, though Philip Whalen and Michael McClure, whom Thomas Parkinson cited for their integrity in 1960, continue to work prodigiously in their old haunts, but even they have of late found working conditions more stimulating in the Rocky Mountains. Whalen shuns the spotlight and refuses to compromise his usually difficult works to court wide favor. McClure has done the most to keep the beat image a conspicuous part of the Bay Area scene with his controversial plays, especially *The Beard* (1965); his appearances in local experimental films and in cameo roles in major commercial films, like Martin Scorsese's *The Last Waltz* (1978), a documentary feature about the breakup of a long-lasting local rock group, The Band; and even by sometimes functioning as historian of the Beat Generation. Lawrence Ferlinghetti still operates the City Lights Bookshop (somewhat expanded) in its original location and on its original principle of offering an all-paperback stock (though his prediction that hardcover books would disappear by 1970 was unfulfilled).[1] Today, however, the busy store has the air of a museum. It has become like Elvis Presley's Graceland—a shrine to which weary but still hopeful pilgrims wend their way from all over the world. They can browse through a stock that despite its diversity still especially features the work of the beats, gone a quarter-century from the store's neighborhood.

Others, however, have been driven out of San Francisco by the constantly rising cost of living. It is not likely that today's Bay Area could host the like of the beats and beatniks; Yuppieland does not promote "the beatific life" on North Beach, especially among "various mendicants."

Since the mass media had been much more interested in the outrageous antics of the beatniks than in the mystical accomplishments of what Ginsberg called "the small circle labeled 'Beat,' "[2] "the only rebellion around" ceased to provide good copy when the tourist-trappers found things more to their taste in Mexico. The last flurry of national publicity for the Beat centered on Michael McClure's efforts from 1965 to 1968 to pro-

duce *The Beard,* but it took the prospect of onstage cunnilingus to rouse the
jaded tastes of sensation-seekers and raise the censors' hackles.[3]

A Fading Frequency: *Pull My Daisy*

During 1960 the conspicuously beat scene shifted across the country
from San Francisco to Greenwich Village and the lively group gathering
around Diane Di Prima and Leroi Jones. This colony was celebrated in
Seymour Krim's *The Beats,* Stanley Fisher's *Beat Coast East,* and Elias
Wilentz's *The Beat Scene,* with photographs by Village denizen Fred
McDarrah (all 1960). Its history, however, has little to do with San Francisco. It is part of a larger New York story, as especially indicated by the ab-
sence of Californians from a major Village Beat book, Leroi Jones's
anthology, *The Moderns* (1963). Although this volume does include
Burroughs and Kerouac, as well as Di Prima and Jones, it does not include
any San Franciscans or even Allen Ginsberg. The others featured are Robert
Creeley, Fielding Dawson, Edward Dorn, William Eastlake, Russel Edsen,
Paul Metcalf, John Rechy, Michael Rumaker, Hubert Selby, Jr., and
Douglas Woolf. (Only Creeley and Rumaker won space in Ann Charters's
The Beats.)

Before leaving the beat scene in other hands, however, Kerouac,
Ginsberg, Orlovsky, and Corso did collaborate with New Yorkers, including painter Larry Rivers and musician David Amram, on one unique project
that, though made in New York, captures perhaps better than any other the
spirit of the San Francisco Poetry Renaissance. Ironically, this swan song,
which might have done much to keep alive the memory and spirit of the
renaissance, has been kept out of circulation for many years because of petty
squabbling.

In 1959 the four beats met with the others in the loft studio of painter
Alfred Leslie on Fourth Avenue in lower Manhattan to shoot a twenty-
eight-minute film, *Pull My Daisy,* based on the third act of Kerouac's
unproduced play *The Beat Generation* and produced and directed by Leslie
and Robert Frank. (In 1969 Frank published *The Americans,* a collection of
his photographs with an introduction that was one of Kerouac's last works.)
The black-and-white 16mm film, shot silently with a superimposed sound-
track ad-libbed by Kerouac (and added later), cost $15,000.

After being enthusiastically received at some film festivals, *Pull My
Daisy* disappeared from circulation because of disputes over distribution
rights; it was not even available to scholars and historians from depositories
like the New York Museum of Modern Art's film library. While it was dif-

ficult in the 1960s to arrange showings of short films in commercial theaters, this one would have been in great demand at the experimental film
programs then popular at many museums and colleges, and audiences
might have gotten some sense of the gently wistful spirit of the beats, in
contrast to the sensational commercialized image of beatniks.

Fortunately, Kerouac's narration was published along with many stills
from the film in 1961, so that it is possible to get a good sense of *Pull My
Daisy,* which is still difficult to get access to in the United States. (I recently
enjoyed seeing it at last in England.)

One can skip the well-intentioned introduction by Jerry Tallmer, who
had known many of those involved in the production and got carried away
by his enthusiasm for it. He called it "an epic poem, a self-appraisal, a sto-
icism," "a plain unvarnished delight," and ended up describing it as a
movement, like Jean Vigo's *Zero de Conduite,* toward "pure film." This is
overblown, and he should have quit after calling it "the most honest and
honestly funny piece of beatthink" within his experience.[4] Such a buildup
can be intimidating, and the reader should trust his or her own individual
response.

There is little plot or action, yet a lot happens in this depiction of one
mad day in the life of a railroad brakeman (obviously modeled on Neal
Cassady, as vividly evoked by Larry Rivers), his wife, who is a painter, and
their grumpy schoolboy son, in whose apartment the beat poets hang out.
This is a special day because a bishop (church unspecified) is coming to call.
Although a loving family, they have the usual disagreements and misunderstandings. The kid doesn't like the farina (shades of Kerouac's own childhood) and doesn't want to go to school; the husband comes home tired and
finally goes off with the boys; the wife is disappointed because the beat visitors have spoiled her efforts to impress the bishop, who has brought his
mother and sister. She thinks "Well, it could have been better because if
Milo wasn't so silly and invited all these silly friends of his, we could have
done some kind of impression for the bishop" (31), and remembers, "All
this time we should have fed them some food, we should have done 'em
some good, we shoulda—all that time you give 'em wine and beer and give
'em all these beatniks in the house" (36). The poets, meanwhile, have been
pleading with the bishop to tell them if things are "holy"—baseball, alliga-
tors, the world, the organ of man, time, the American flag, the bishop himself? The bishop can only reply, "I see that, I think it's best that I go now
and go make my holy offices (laughs) if you know what I mean" (24).

The rambling narration and the snatches of conversation perfectly exemplify what Ferlinghetti called "street poetry"—a medium that communi-

cates with families like Milo's better than did the Depression-era agitprop effort to create a people's poetry out of ideological slogans. The narration is also an illustration of Kerouac's concept of "unconditioned mind," as suggested by his opening line: "Early morning in the universe"—the characters are everybody (21). This is drama akin to Thornton Wilder's *Our Town*, but set far from a greeting-card pretty New England village and in a grubby apartment on Manhattan's East Side instead.

There is no *message* of any kind. Instead of making a statement, Kerouac posed a question that might be phrased, "If ordinary people of good will have so much trouble communicating with each other, what can be expected of efforts to talk between larger and varied cultural groups conditioned to change the world to their personal desires?" Instead of puzzling out another intellectual abstraction of academic art, one is invited to participate in the scene. Here is the place to begin to get on the beat frequency. It is regrettable that this doorway has been blocked for so long.

Meanwhile, Back in San Francisco

The New York Beat pursued its own path. The title *Beatitude* had been lured back from its Eastern captivity to its starting place in San Francisco, where it was employed spasmodically by a number of editors representing a changing poetic constitutency. It is not even certain how many issues appeared between numbers 17 and 33, since guides to serials and little magazines make no reference at all to many intervening numbers.

The silver anniversary issue of 1985 could have been numbered 33 only symbolically; it is a far cry from the original collections of mimeographed pages stapled together. With its carefully typeset and tastefully printed pages, profusely interlarded with illustrations and slick photographs of many contributors, this issue gives the impression that the money changers have set up in the temple again. Editor Jeffrey Grossman did provide a fragmentary history of what had happened since the last copy from the Bread and Wine Mission appeared in 1960: "Later in the 60s revitalized by Stephen Schwartz, aided financially by Shig Murao [of City Lights Bookshop and *Howl* trial fame]. Then again in the 70s by Luke Breit, Raymond Faye, Neeli Cherkovski and Jack Hirschman. Since then Tisa Walden edited two. Other editions by H. D. Moe, Ken Wainer, Kristen Wetterhahn and Nate May."[5] (None of these individuals, including Grossman, are identified in Ann Charters's *The Beats*.)

Few figures from the old poetry renaissance were back for the anniversary celebration. Of the original contributors to *Beatitude*, Kerouac's 1959 letter to Harpo Marx was reprinted—"Was your vow of silence an Indian koan?" (3); Gregory Corso contributed a group containing a drawing, a photograph, and "Love Poem"; David Meltzer contributed "The Red Shoes," a collection of familiar clichés about dancing through San Francisco streets; Michael McClure was represented by a poem for Ginsberg, with a photograph of the two of them; and Ginsberg turned up again in a photograph with Shig Murao, accompanying two 1979–80 poems, the latter "Verses Written for Student Antidraft Registration Rally 1980." There were also poems by other readers from the 1955 program at the Six Gallery—Philip Lamantia, Gary Snyder, and Philip Whalen—and some haiku by Ruth Weiss. The issue closed with Bob Kaufman's "A Buddhist Experience."

Among the many included in the twenty-fifth anniversary issue who had not contributed to the original magazine, so far as is known, were Harold Norse, Jack Micheline, Ted Joans, William Everson, and editor Grossman, who rhapsodizes about "The Perfect Hamburger" in a series of cute images that have none of the original beat intensity. Many former contributors did turn up as cosigners of a "Pact between America and Viet Nam" with Roshi Trungpa, Li Po, Muktananda, and Amour LeKa. The editor had the last word: "People seem to have personal reasons for whatever they do. I must find my motives" (239)—a message hardly on the old beat frequency but one that turns up increasingly often in the later work of those who seem driven to write without knowing why. If this huge and unremarkable assemblage of the works of 127 writers is San Francisco's last word on the poetry renaissance it fostered, one must clearly look elsewhere for signs of continuing vitality.

The Outsider Way Down Yonder

The most pretentious effort to promote the beat cause (if there could be said to be one) after the breakup of the San Francisco camp was a stimulating but short-lived one in New Orleans's Vieux Carré (French Quarter), beginning in 1961. Little mention has been made of the Louisiana city thus far. Though it was one of the dynamic centers of the blooming of modernist American literature in the 1920s—when William Faulkner, Sherwood Anderson, and the *Double Dealer* were enjoying the best escape the country offered during the puritanical prohibition era—by the 1950s the city had salvaged itself out of the general somnolence of the South by becoming a tourist trap. The powerful figure dominating local literary culture was Frances Parkinson Keyes, then one of the nation's most consistently bestselling authors. Her long, leisurely blends of carefully researched history and colorful romance were popular with an older generation that still prided itself on reading books but deplored the vulgarity of most contemporary writing. Keyes had settled in the French Quarter during World War II and made the Quarter, the city, and the region the subjects of many of her most admired works, like *Steamboat Gothic* (1952). The Beat could hardly have been expected to strongly penetrate the territory that this formidable socialite ruled from her mansion (now the Beauregard-Keyes House) on rue Chartres near rue Ursuline in the most respectable lower Quarter.

But the beats could try. Only a few blocks away, the traditional painters of land- and seascapes and jungle beasts on velvet hawked their wares in Pirate's Alley and around Jackson Square, eking out a living from the tourists who knew what they liked. (Fauve-influenced modernists were looked at askance by both these visiting middle-class tourists and the still reigning Creole aristocracy of old French and Spanish families.) Even the traditional New Orleans music was disappearing as the Bourbon Street hangouts of the B-girls became increasingly sleazy. As historian E. L. Borenstein observed, "To the visiting jazz enthusiast looking for live traditional music in New Orleans the period 1957 to 1960 was a rough one."[6]

But the times were changing. In 1957 the owner of Associated Artists Studio, a small gallery at 726 rue St. Peter, began encouraging older musicians still in the area to drop in on their way to Pat O'Brien's popular bar. Grayson Mills, a young jazz fan from California, turned up to record some sessions and then returned in 1961 to set up a regular program managed by Allan and Sandy Jaffe in the old gallery, now renamed Preservation Hall (the gallery itself moved next door). New Orleans jazz was on its way back and thrives to this day; every night there is a long line of jazz lovers trying to get into Preservation Hall. Pilgrims have traveled to New Orleans from all over the world, though most of the local action has now moved away from the Bourbon Street honky-tonks to night spots like Tipitina's, a St. Charles streetcar ride away.

In the early 1960s a determined couple began an effort to bring New Orleans back into the literary avant-garde and set up just around the corner from Preservation Hall on Rue Royale, in one of the nineteenth-century buildings with the most glorious wrought-iron balconies. They would shortly move a few blocks south to rue Ursuline, just down the street from the Keyes house.

Jon Edgar Webb and his wife Gypsy Lou turned out only three issues of *The Outsider* on their painfully slow handpress—just one each year from 1961 to 1963. They had originally planned to publish a quarterly but claimed in the first issue that it had taken 4,500 hours to turn it out. Although they made no statement of editorial policy, the beats predominated in this issue. Included were works of Ray Bremser, William Burroughs, Gregory Corso, Diane Di Prima, Allen Ginsberg, Leroi Jones, "Mike" McClure, Barbara Moraff, Peter Orlovsky, Jory Sherman, and Gary Snyder, along with the works of many who frequently appeared with the beats— Cid Corman, Robert Creeley, Judson Crews, Edward Dorn, Lawrence Ferlinghetti, Langston Hughes, Henry Miller, Charles Olson, Gilbert Sorrentino, Jonathan Williams, and Colin Wilson, the Britisher whose provocative book provided the name of the magazine. There also appeared some of the seemingly alienated Los Angelenos—James Boyer May, Gene Frumkin, and Leslie Woolf Hedley; no one from Rexroth's San Francisco group was in the first issue. Also included was "A Charles Bukowski Album," six pages from the work of the poet who was to be the subject of the Webbs' most spectacular production, *It Catches My Heart in Its Hands* (1963). Prepublication autographed copies of this volume, handprinted on a Fauvist rainbow of colored papers, were offered for two dollars.

The opulence of this edition and the even more elaborate *Crucifix in a Deathhead,* another Bukowski collection they prepared for a New York publisher in 1965, gives one an unshakable feeling that the Webbs intended to create museum pieces. The Webbs were not themselves creative writers but appreciative curators, and their productions signaled a shift in the treatment of the beats and Bukowski from their ephemeral presentation in mimeographed bulletins and flimsy chapbooks to their preservation in what would become treasured memorials—an extraordinary show of confidence in writers others tended to denounce.

The second issue confirms the impression that the Webbs were preserving history rather than making it. It offers many of the same contributors as the first, along with Jack Kerouac, Philip Lamantia, Larry Eigner, William J. Margolis, Jack Micheline, Jean Genet, Kenneth Patchen, Mason Jordan Mason, and, surprisingly, Howard Nemerov, who from his academic stronghold attacked

> The sponsors, fund raisers, and members of the board,
> Who naturally assume their seats among the governors,
> and asking
>   . . . are they not as ourselves in these things also?
>   . . . the orphan, the pauper, the thief, the derelict drunk.[7]

There are no such surprising entries in the third issue, and fewer new voices—only poems by Carl Solomon and a very young Diane Wakowski and a story by old-timer Willard Motley. The "Outsider of the Year" was Charles Bukowski, and a large feature was devoted to a "jazz documentary" on the history of New Orleans music and the attempt to revive it begun in the previous issue.

The Outsider was far more ambitious than most publications with beat affinities. All three of the New Orleans issues ran over one hundred pages. At the end of the decade the even more ambitious Winter 1968–69 double issue appeared from Tucson, Arizona, as a two-hundred-page hardback, but few contributors harked back to the poetry renaissance, except Lenore Kandel, identified as living and writing in Hawaii. Much of this issue was devoted to tributes to Kenneth Patchen, and the editorials were almost exclusively concerned with efforts to keep the perilous venture afloat. "Unless something quite unexpected comes our way, a substantial grant or a private subsidy, this Number 4/5 issue is *The Outsider's* last," a long "Editor's Bit & Obit." began; the masthead announced, "Sold home & workshop to help put this issue out—must move." Where to is not known—*The Outsider* was not heard from again.

Its three New Orleans issues provide insight into the difficulties of establishing a sense of continuity for a phenomenon like the San Francisco Poetry Renaissance; the public had lost interest in it in order to pursue trendy new fads, and there seemed to be no concern whether anything of value was lost in this restless quest. The American mass media are like Tom and Daisy Buchanan of Scott Fitzgerald's *The Great Gatsby:* "careless people [who] smashed up things and creatures and then retreated back into their money, their vast carelessness . . . and let other people clean up the mess they had made" (Chapter 9).

The Webbs exhausted themselves and their resources in a doomed effort to attract a larger and more affluent audience for their wares by resorting to the kind of elaborate gimmicks that appeal to audiences that do not remain long devoted to one cause. The carnival atmosphere of New Orleans was not one in which the serious beats—or even Kenneth Rexroth and his followers—were likely to flourish.

Beat Archives

At just about the same time that the Webbs were pursuing their gloriously misguided course, leaving us with treasures from which they never benefited—except in the day-to-day pleasure that their activities must have given them, despite their complaints—the beats were beginning to receive some serious scholarly attention.

Talk of beat archives is ludicrous because there are scarcely any. The notable exception is the Harris Collection of American Poetry and Plays in the John Hay Library at Brown University, which has been somewhat erratically developed on the idea of its patron, that an attempt should be made to assemble a *complete* archive of the American platform arts and that selection of materials should not be based on the preconceived notions of any one party about what *should* be included in such a collection.

In November 1962 Brown held what was apparently the first major exhibition of beat poetry, "3 Beat Poets," compiled from a collection of books and manuscripts largely from the Harris Collection. At that time even a mention of the disreputable beatniks was anathema in most polite American establishments. To the bibliography distributed at this "first exhibition" of works of Gregory Corso, Lawrence Ferlinghetti, and Allen Ginsberg, someone contributed a short unsigned statement of incredible perceptiveness: "It may also be the last time that the poets may be exhibited or associated together as 'Beat poets,' for each has found his own voice regardless of a literary group or school. . . . The writings of . . . their early creative years are exhibited to show that the Beat movement has left us a substantial body of serious poetry."

What is interesting about this statement is the assumption that the beats as a group, like the earlier fauves, had split up and that each had moved on after finding an individual voice. What can hardly be expected from a judgment made at that time—when the beats were still thriving nearby in New York—is any thoroughgoing recognition that their "substantial body of serious poetry" might well have reflected a sensibility that extended beyond individuals, or that the beats, unlike the fauves standing on the brink of sensational breakthroughs in their art, were voices of the last significant American avant-garde movement that would develop from literary origins to find literary expression. Something more than a lone exhibit at Brown was required to perceive the significance of the beats. It was a long time coming.

The beats would have to undergo a period of eclipse because, as has been stressed, they were not ideologists or activists, and the nation was being pushed into a period of activism. The Beat shifted elsewhere. It remained active in England, at the Beat Hotel in Paris, and elsewhere in Europe; but consideration of these developments is beyond the limits of this study. The United States had to undergo Vietnam. In its disastrous wake, the beats' voices would be heard again. What the beats wrote during the years of the agitation over the war was largely ignored at the time, but their work proved to be much more than nostalgia.

In 1968 and 1969, respectively, Neal Cassady and Jack Kerouac died deplorable deaths. The times were ripening for martyrology, but it was 1971 before the appearance of Bruce Cook's book *The Beat Generation,* which principally related the good old days with Kerouac, Ginsberg, and Burroughs in New York. Much more important to archiving the history of the beats was the publication, also in 1971, of the first three issues of *the unspeakable visions of the individual* by Arthur Knight and his wife, Glee, who also died tragically when she was only twenty-seven. The first important volume in the series was *The Beat Book* (1974), prepared for publication before Glee's death. With his later wife, Kit, Knight produced ten more volumes between 1977 and 1985. Meanwhile, things happening elsewhere assured not just the memorializing of the San Francisco poetry renaissance but a lively effort to regenerate its spirit in a new generation.

Naropa

Allen Ginsberg spent much of the early 1960s in far-flung travels in search of his own identity—first to South American jungles for the vision-inducing drug *yage,* and then to the Far East. These varied experiences had a strong impact on Ginsberg's highly impressionable sensibility, and he underwent a basic change in his attitude toward existence while in Japan. He recorded this experience in his poem "The Change: Kyoto-Tokyo Express" (1963). As Thomas F. Merrill described the experience, Ginsberg "found that the object of his quest was not something outside himself—the complete consciousness that Death seemed to promise—but rather his own heart within. . . . It meant renouncing virtually all of his previous commitments," even Blake. Merrill described the poem itself as "not remarkable," but concluded, "The message is succinct but repetitive: no more visions; live in the skin and the present time."[8]

A formal commitment to Buddhism, Merrill pointed out, meant a shift from a "theistic" base (Judeo-Christian) to a "nontheistic" one (12). During the mid-1960s Ginsberg's turning inward toward greater self-examination led to a period of political activism and extensive publication, resulting in his arrests in Prague in 1965 and at the Republican National Convention in Miami in 1972. As the American political situation deteriorated following the Vietnam debacle and the Watergate scandals, Ginsberg, like Robert Bly and others, searched again for a more quietist position.

In 1971, the same year that Philip Whalen joined the Zen Center in San Francisco to become a Buddhist monk, Ginsberg met the guru who was to exercise the greatest influence on his lifestyle and thought, Tibetan lama

Chogyam Trungpa. In 1973 Ginsberg studied under Trungpa at the Naropa Seminary in Jackson Hole, Wyoming; as Merrill explained, he was exploring *not* Zen, but a form of Tibetan meditation known as "simple *samatha,*" which, Ginsberg explained is a Sanskrit word meaning "pacification . . . tranquilization of mind style" (124, ellipsis in text).

Enjoying an unpretentious lifestyle, Ginsberg felt tranquilized enough for the calling for which he seemed destined—that of teacher—so that when Trungpa went to Boulder, Colorado, to realize "his dream of creating a college which would combine contemplative studies with traditional Western scholastic and artistic disciplines," Ginsberg was willing to join him.[9] Before turning up at Naropa, however, he joined Orlovsky, Corso, McClure, Snyder, Ferlinghetti, Murao, a reconciled or vanquished Rexroth, and Miriam Patchen (by then a widow) during the blizzardy week of 18 March 1974 in Grand Forks, North Dakota. They were there for the Fifth Annual University of North Dakota Writers Conference, "City Lights in North Dakota," the first of several tributes to the poetry renaissance that would take place as American academia reconciled itself to the survivors. (Although reporter James McKenzie would recall that not long before the English Department of Jersey City State College made a public issue of not endorsing a reading there by Ginsberg.)[10]

Enter Anne Waldman   In building a program in writing and poetics, featuring an especially strong summer offering, Ginsberg needed dynamic and experienced help, administration had never been a beat strong point. To provide this, Trungpa recruited Anne Waldman in 1975 as cofounder of the program, whose direction she has remained principally active in ever since. (Ginsberg usually participates in the summer program but spends much of the rest of the year back in New York.) Waldman was born in April 1945—a year after Ginsberg, Kerouac, and Burroughs met in New York—in nearby southern New Jersey and moved with her parents to MacDougal Street in Greenwich Village after World War II. In a lecture on her life at Naropa, she explained that she first began to read the beats in Donald Allen's anthology when she was fifteen, just as the Beat was shifting from San Francisco to New York. This discovery led her to books by Ginsberg, Denise Levertov, Robert Creeley, and Frank O'Hara, John Ashbery, and Kenneth Koch of the New York School of poets and painters.[11] After attending Bennington College, where she studied with Howard Nemerov and Bernard Malamud and wrote her senior thesis on Theodore Roethke, she went to California for the Berkeley Poetry Conference in 1965, then returned to New York, where in 1968 she became director of the St. Mark's Poetry Project in the Village. She remained there until 1977. Her first book of poems, *On the Wing,* had appeared in 1968. Ginsberg heard her at public readings in New York, and Ferlinghetti published her sixth collection, *Fast Speaking Woman,* in the City Lights Pocket Poets Series that had launched many of the beats. They encouraged her in a career that earned her an international reputation through her readings at festivals abroad.

Then in 1974 she was invited to join Ginsberg and her friend Diane Di Prima at the Naropa summer workshop in "Spontaneous Poetics." This was so successful that Trungpa was encouraged to organize a permanent school as part of his project; in 1975 Ginsberg and Waldman established the Jack Kerouac School of Disembodied Poetics, modeled after the former Black Mountain College, which both admired. Waldman's talents as a performer, reader, and teacher and her fund-raising abilities have made her an indispensible asset to the program, which "places an emphasis on clear and and attentive oral presentation of works, since it is as speech that words proclaim themselves and communicate fully."[12]

Waldman's position at Naropa has brought her into closer collaboration with veterans of the San Francisco Poetry Renaissance than any other poet of the next generation. One of the most ambitious and attractive publications of this group since Naropa has made a large contribution to rekindling interest in it is *Five/1/77,* a portfolio of broadsides of poems and drawings prepared by the poets for lithographing and hand-printing in 1977. It affords a particularly interesting opportunity to compare the work of this younger poet with four founders of the renaissance.

Gregory Corso's contribution, "Clone," is an upbeat mingling of words and marginal drawings that makes the characteristically insouciant point that when the gods object to the speaker's giving away sky, trees, and seas, he gives the gods away. Ginsberg's "The Rune" is a song written at Ken Kesey's piano on 13 May 1977 at a contest of bards. It makes a romantic statement in line with his Buddhist viewpoint: "When the years have gone," we die, not still wanting Earth, "But return, where all the beauties rest." Michael McClure's "Politics Starts with a Barrel of Arson," presented in his familiar style of juxtaposing boldly printed assertions, makes the cumulative point that "We are the heroes of our problems." Philip Whalen's "For Clark Coolidge" (a New York poet) is difficult to summarize or even comprehend, as is often the case with his work, because of complicated allusions to philanthropists and advertisers—"Clara Wilkes Booth, founderess / Red Cross and Salvation Army / Clara Barton Batten Durstine and Osburn." It concludes, after the speaker's pause for a scotch, with only the word *sham.* I dwell on these poems selected with obvious care for this unusual collection, to show how, when involved in such a project, the poets returned to forms and subjects they had frequently used twenty years earlier, though Ginsberg's tone has mellowed a bit. The poems all stress concrete physical objects intended to arouse strong emotions.

Anne Waldman's dialogue between a male sun-lover and a female moon-lover ends with both saying, "only the word sings"—a much more abstract and intellectual concept than the ideas presented in the other poems. It is dangerous to generalize from a single example about the reason for this difference; but it is thought-provoking to find that of all these poets it was the younger Waldman who having grown up in a postmodernist literary milieu, put particular emphasis on the act of writing and on writing about writing and who distrusted generalizations about connections between words and their referents. This specimen of her work chosen for a very special collaboration exemplifies the characteristic impersonality and abstractness of much post–World War II writing. It suggests a basis, for example, for worried responses like Norman Podhoretz's to "primitivism and spontaneity." Significantly, Waldman has listed among activities prominent in her work in the early 1980s making list-poems and collages in William Burroughs's manner (533)—activities that use words as things in themselves rather than as referents. One may speculate that in being run by Waldman and Ginsberg the program benefits from a generational tension between emphases on coolness and intensity and that this tension may keep it from succumbing to the principal danger facing such programs: becoming academic museums for the veneration and preservation of past practices.

The Jack Kerouac School of Disembodied Poetics

Certainly the name chosen for the program, the Jack Kerouac School of Disembodied Poetics, brings to mind this danger by being almost self-parodically ghost-haunted. According to Ann Charters, Waldman chose the name in 1975 because she thought it would be "playful and 'tantric,' " but she had come to regret it because critics attacked the word *disembodied* as nonsense (531). It is not nonsense at all, with its implication of the authority of a dead hand, but the word is perhaps inadvisable because it puts too much emphasis on an unworldliness that was already causing critics and neighbors some misgivings about Naropa. It may be significant that, after Trungpa's departure, the summer 1989 announcement described the program as having been founded with this title, in small print at the bottom but called in the "Summer Writing Program" in bold type in the eye-catching notice at the top.

This danger of getting mired in the past—as the fauves, for example, never did—is suggested by an advertisement in Ferlinghetti's *City Lights Journal* for the school's 1978 faculty: Imamu Amiri Baraka, Michael Brownstein, William Burroughs, Gregory Corso, Robert Duncan, Allen Ginsberg, Ken Kesey, Michael McClure, Ed Sanders, John Wieners, Anne Waldman, and two women with unfamiliar names. Certainly anyone asking in 1978, "Where did the old beats go?" would need only be referred to this prospectus.

Not everything has been smooth skiing for this institution on the slopes of the Rockies. Serious friction between Naropa and the community threatened to involve the writing program after an unpleasant incident in 1975 involving visiting poet W. S. Merwin and his female companion, Dana Naone. Accounts of the matter vary greatly, but there seems to be general agreement that the visitors became involved in some advanced rituals from which neophytes were usually excluded. Merwin claimed that he and his companion had been embarrassed and humiliated, and the local press took his side in demanding an investigation. Trungpa and his associates maintained that the visitors did not understand the ritualistic significance of their treatment. No one appeared satisfied that Merwin's complaints were adequately answered, and the matter remained a bone of contention as late as 1979, when Tom Clark wrote his account of it, embittering many residents of Boulder and poets internationally against Naropa. The writing program became involved because Merwin had been invited as its guest; the incident in question, however, had no direct connection with the school; it happened at Snowmass, a seminary for advanced students of tantric Buddhism operated separately by Trungpa at a remote ski lodge.[13]

Attention was at last diverted from this disquieting episode by the mellowest and most highly publicized production at the school in its early years, the Naropa conference celebrating the twenty-fifth anniversary of the publication of Jack Kerouac's *On the Road*, held during the last week of July 1982. The occasion brought together, besides lesser-known well-wishers, Allen Ginsberg, Ray Bremser, William Burroughs, Carolyn Cassady, Gregory Corso, Diane Di Prima, Lawrence Ferlinghetti, John Clellon Holmes, Hubert Huncke, Paul Krassner (longtime editor of the beat-sympathetic *Realist*), Fran and Jay Landesman (founders of *Neurotica*), Joanna and Michael McClure, and Carl Solomon, The conference also had some somewhat surprising attendees—Abbie Hoffman, Ken Kesey and Ken Babbs of Merry Pranksters fame, Robert LaVigne (the artist who had introduced Ginsberg and Peter Orlovsky), Timothy Leary (with whom

Ginsberg and Kerouac had participated in drug experiments in the early 1960s), and John Steinbeck, the novelist's son.

Also among those present was a breed whose very existence might not have been anticipated in 1957—not beat historians, but historians of the Beat: Ann and Samuel Charters, Arthur and Kit Knight, Gerald Nicosia, and John Tytell. By the time of the conference there were not only histories and biographies but, in the United States, a journal devoted to the beats, *Moody Street Irregulars* (named for one of Kerouac's childhood haunts in Lowell, Massachusetts), edited by Joy Walsh since 1978. It would be joined in 1984 by a "Beat Brotherhood Newsletter," *The Kerouac Connection,* edited by Dave Moore in Bristol, England.

The beats, in fact, enjoy an even more enthusiastic following today in Great Britain and Europe, where more young people are inclined toward reading, than in the United States. Local fans, including many college students, joined Carolyn Cassady, Joy Walsh, Gerald Nicosia, Dave Moore, and others in Plymouth, England, on 6-7 June 1987 for "Beat Dreams, Plymouth Sounds," a conference highlighted by an evening performance by Slim Gaillard, one of Kerouac's favorite jazz artists. It also coincided with the release of a new anthology, *The Beats* by Park Honan of the University of Leeds, where another conference is being contemplated. In addition, a touring group has performed the City Lights Show at several venues in England.

Meanwhile, the situation at Naropa has become destabilized in a manner that makes the writing of this account particularly appropriate at a time when the perseverance of the spirit of the San Francisco Poetry Renaissance is uncertain. Unexpectedly, on 4 April 1987, Chogyam Trungpa died at the age of forty-seven (the same age at which, Jack Kerouac had died eighteen years earlier). Possibly anticipating such an eventuality, Naropa had appointed a new chancellor, Barbara Dilley, creator at the founding of the institute's dance program. The staff and supporting community were dismayed, however, when the sponsoring organization, Shambhala Training, an international network of programs offering meditation training to the general public, announced that it was withdrawing from the Boulder institute and moving its headquarters for the Western Hemisphere to Halifax, Nova Scotia, taking 150 members of the local Buddhist community with it. The director of Karma Dzong, the local church, expected about five hundred of its one thousand members to remain in Boulder. An anonymous donor provided a gift to keep the institute going, but Ginsberg was shocked to hear that one of the offerings would be a conference on "Spiritual Values in Business."

Scandal followed when the news broke that Orel Tendzin, whom Trungpa named as his successor in the Vajradhatu network of meditation centers, was suspended after it was learned he had been infected with AIDS since 1985, although he did not acknowledge his condition until 1988, when a male companion and a female friend were also found to be infected. Tendzin, who had been born Thomas F. Rich,—by ironic coincidence, in Ginsberg's home town of Passaic, New Jersey—had aggravated matters by insisting upon maintaining his teaching and ceremonial duties in defiance of a request by the movement's board of directors.[14]

The community, however, has continued to support Naropa, which is planning a $3 million expansion that it is hoped will increase the student body from four hundred to six hundred in the next century. The institute, now identified only as "Buddhist-oriented," is also planning a new mental health center in conjunction with Boulder County.[15]

The 1989 flier for the summer writing program already lists a greatly expanded faculty of at least thirty-six. Some familiar names are present to give it the stamp of tradition—William Burroughs, Diane Di Prima, Clark Coolidge, and Michael McClure, along with a celebrity visitor, British artist David Hockney, who provided a focal point for the program. Most of the faculty, however, have yet to make their reputations. It seems possible that the institute has indeed broken loose from its thralldom to the dead. According to Allen Ginsberg, "It continues to cook."[16]

How Important Was the San Francisco Poetry Renaissance?

I have already suggested that the answer to Thomas Parkinson's early question appears to be that the beats were indeed a phenomenon rather than a generation. The Beat was like the fauve breakthrough it in many ways paralleled: an electrifying shock treatment that jolted a culture into some transformation of a moribund lifestyle but that did not produce a legacy of masterpieces.

In 1970, just a decade after the renaissance went to pot, as it were, the Beats were being forgotten in a wave of youthful activism and were much less celebrated than they are now two decades later, when they have taken on a glow like that radiating from Fauvist paintings in another colorless time. At the time, I was editing a collection of essays on the American literature of the 1950s and asked Kingsley Widmer, a leading authority on twentieth-century American bohemianism and literary censorship, to write a retrospective appreciation of the beats. What he wrote then remains, I feel, generally valid and provides the most appropriate summing up of a movement that remains a generative force in American life.[17]

Widmer concluded his general survey of the beats: "In its largest ambitions, Beat literature presents a personal entree into the process of apocalyptic vision. It prophesies and demonstrates, by idiosyncrasies and hysterias, against a dehumanizing and exploitative technocratic civilization—bomb-ridden, consumer-compulsive, competitively anxious, sensually confused, mass-media warped, institutionally boxed, politically mad—and therefore incapable of simplicity and contemplation and intense experience and tenderness and community and love. And surely doomed!" (159).[18]

Noting that "with the one main exception of Allen Ginsberg, it is hard to identify major progenitors of Beat poeticism" (166), Widmer pointed out that "there could hardly be a *good* anthology of Beat poetry as such" (168).

He contended, however, that "the Beats appear to have had a considerable, perhaps even disproportionate, effect on American sensibility and life styles" (171).

The main significance of the Beat movement of the 50s, I believe, was not literary but cultural in a far broader sense. In attempting to change the bland bureaucratic-technological society by transforming sensibility and trying to radically revitalize a false order by creating a different life-style, the movement was toward a cultural revolution. The new populist culture contained considerable malaise: adolescent addiction—and addictive adolescence—but also rather synthetic religiosity, morality replaced by relativistic muddle, a decline in artist craftsmanship in the name of self-expression, and an often naively ineffective politics of rebelliousness and tenderness. But the movement itself, and our need for it, remains considerably greater than its obvious failings (173).

As it still does.

Notes and References

Preface

1. Arthur Winfield Knight, *"the unspeakable visions of the individual:* A History," *Kerouac Connection* 12 (November 1986), 9.
2. I have examined seven of the first fifteen issues of *Beatitude,* but I have not located a complete file. I have not located any file of *Underhound,* and it is not mentioned in most writings about the beats in San Francisco. The best available information about it comes from C. V. J. Anderson's "North Beach Strikes a Blow for Freedom," an undated tearsheet from *Dorian Book Quarterly,* a sales catalog from a San Francisco gay bookstore. It identifies Anderson as the co-founder with Alan Dienstag of *Underhound* in October 1959. Jory Sherman (a poet discussed in chapter 3) sent me this clipping with others used in this study in May 1960.

Introduction

1. Six essays containing material for a history of the San Francisco Renaissance comprised a special feature in *Literary Review* 32, no. 1 (Fall 1988): Linda Hamalian, "The Genesis of the San Francisco Renaissance: Literary and Political Currents, 1945–1955," 5–8; Lee Bartlett, "From Waldport to San Francisco: Art and Politics Make Peace," 9–15; Thomas Parkinson, "The Poets Take Over: New Forums for Literature in the Bay Area," 16–20; Herbert Blau, "From Red Hill to the Renaissance: Rehearsing the Resistance," 21–28; James Schevill, "Mirrors for a 'Renaissance,' " 29–34; and Diane Wakowski, "The Birth of the San Francisco: Something Now Called the Whitman Tradition," 35–42.
2. Quoted in Paul Krassner, "High Noon at Camp Kerouac," *The Beat Road (unspeakable visions of the individual,* Vol. 14) (1984), 11.
3. Allen Ginsberg, *Howl and Other Poems* (San Francisco: City Lights Books, 1956), 12.
4. Thomas Parkinson, ed., *A Casebook on the Beat* (New York: Thomas Y. Crowell, 1961), 279–80.
5. In a long 23 August 1958 interview in New York with United Press International, Kerouac said, "There is no relation between the pranks of that lonesome, talkative beat generation of the '40s and the concerted desecrations of this new delinquency-hounded generation of the '50s" (Quoted in *Kerouac Connection,* no. 14 [Summer 1987], 13). For comments by Corso and Ginsberg, see the last two paragraphs of Chapter 1.
6. William Hogan, "A Few Cool Words for *Howl,*" *San Francisco Chronicle,* May 1957 (unspecified date), reprinted in *Coastlines,* no. 8 (Autumn 1957), 34.
7. My interpretive criticism of *Howl* appears in *Reference Guide to American*

Literature, 2d ed., ed. D. L. Kirkpatrick (Chicago and London: St. James Press, 1987), 643–44.

Chapter One

1. Jack Kerouac, *The Dharma Bums* (New York: Viking Press, 1958), 14.
2. "Beatitude," *Beatitude Anthology* (San Francisco: City Lights Books, 1960).
3. Ibid.
4. Kenneth Rexroth, "Disengagement: The Art of the Beat Generation," *New World Writing,* no. 11 (May 1957), 40; reprinted in *The Beat Generation and the Angry Young Men,* eds. Gene Feldman and Max Gartenberg (New York: Citadel Press, 1958). The term had appeared in *New World Writing,* no. 7 (April 1955), in "Jazz of the Beat Generation" by "Jean-Louis"—identified as a selection from his novel in progress then titled *The Beat Generation*—but it attracted little attention. "Jean-Louis" was not identified as Kerouac until an index to all previous issues appeared in no. 11. The selection does not appear in this form in *On the Road,* though passages from it appear there nonconsecutively.
5. Seymour Krim, ed., *The Beats* (Greenwich, Conn.: Gold Medal Books, 1960), 1.
6. Collioure, often described as only a fishing village, is a Phoenician-Roman fortress that was the main port of the medieval kingdom of Mallorca. It contains many historic structures, including a royal castle and church with a great baroque altar, and it has long been an artist's colony with many galleries.
7. See John Elderfield, *The Wild Beasts: Fauvism and Its Affinities* (New York: Museum of Modern Art, 1976), 43, for a debunking of the myth that the label was derisive. In discussing the fauves, I generally follow Elderfield's most insightful history (hereafter cited in text), though analogies between the fauves and the beats are entirely my own.
8. Reproduced in color in Elderfield, 40.
9. Jack Kerouac, "Biographical Resume," *Heaven and Other Poems* (Bolinas, Calif.: Grey Fox Press, 1977), 39–40. A fictionalized version of these events appears in Kerouac's *Vanity of Duluoz* (New York: Putnam's, 1968), 151.
10. Tim Hunt, *Kerouac's Crooked Road: Development of a Fiction* (Hamden, Conn.: Archon Books, 1981) provides a detailed account of Kerouac's efforts at developing the desired form for fictionalizing his experiences with Neal Cassady.
11. Those days are recounted in biographies of Kerouac—especially Gerald Nicosia, *Memory Babe: A Critical Biography of Jack Kerouac* (New York: Grove Press, 1983)—Allen Ginsberg, and William Burroughs, and in general histories such as Bruce Cook, *The Beat Generation* (New York: Scribner's, 1971) and John Tytell, *Naked Angels: The Lives and Literature of the Beat Generation* (New York: McGraw-Hill, 1976).
12. John Clellon Holmes, *Go* (New York: Scribner's, 1952), 166.
13. Richard Kirk Ardinger, "John Clellon Holmes," in *The Beats: Literary*

Bohemianism in Postwar America, ed. Ann Charters, Dictionary of Literary Biography 16 (Detroit: Bruccoli/Clark-Gale Research, 1983), 251; hereafter referred to as Charters, *The Beats.*

14. John Clellon Holmes, "Jay and Fran Landesman," in Charters, *The Beats,* 339. The nine issues of *Neurotica* have been twice collected and reprinted in book form: *The Compleat Neurotica,* eds. Jay Landesman and Gershon Legman (New York: Hacker Art Books, 1963) and *Neurotica 1948–1951,* ed. Jay Landesman (London: Jay Landesman Ltd., 1981).

15. The term derives from Robert M. Lindner's book *Rebel without a Cause* (New York: Grune and Stratton, 1944), a true case history of a juvenile delinquent. Ray used hardly anything from the book but the title. He met with Lindner, but they disagreed totally about the film (see John Francis Kreidl, *Nicholas Ray* [Boston: Twayne, 1977], especially 87–90). Ray's conception and James Dean's portrayal of the "rebel" was a tremendous hit with restless teenagers and did much to shape the response to the beatniks, especially after Dean's sensational death, when he became a legendary cult hero.

16. John Clellon Holmes, "All the Good Roles Have Been Taken—The Plight of the Talented Untalented," *Neurotica* (1948), 32.

17. Holmes, "Jay and Fran Landesman," 339.

18. Gershon Legman, *Love and Death: A Study in Censorship* (New York: Breaking Point, 1949), 8–9.

19. Gershon Legman, *The Fake Revolt* (New York: Breaking Point, 1967), 4–5, 31.

20. "A Statement by Kenneth Patchen," *Coastlines* 9 (Winter 1957–58), 46.

21. Reproduced in *The Beat Diary (unspeakable visions of the individual* 5) (1977), 8.

22. Henry Miller, preface to Jack Kerouac, *The Subterraneans* (New York: Avon, 1959).

23. For a discussion of Allen's "little man," see Nancy Pogel, *Woody Allen* (Boston: Twayne, 1987), especially 17–31.

24. For an evaluation of Miller as an artist and a self-made myth, see Kingsley Widmer, *Henry Miller Revisited* (Boston: Twayne, 1990). Widmer concluded that Miller is at his best as a clown parodying the conspicuous consumption of the American middle class, and at his worst when, as also happened in Chaplin's and Allen's work, the clown attempts to become a tragic philosopher.

25. *The Outsider* 1 (Fall 1961), 91.

26. Ibid., 79.

27. *The Outsider* 2 (Summer 1962), 47.

28. Legman, *The Fake Revolt,* 32.

29. Donald Hall, "The New Poetry: Notes on the Past Fifteen Years," *New World Writing* 7 (April 1955), 246.

30. "First Reading at the Six Gallery, October 7, 1955," Appendix 2 to *Howl, Original Draft Facsimile,* ed. Barry Miles (New York: Harper & Row,

1986), 165–68, reprints accounts of the evening by Allen Ginsberg and Gregory Corso in *The Literary Revolution in America,* by Jack Kerouac in *The Dharma Bums,* and by Ginsberg and Peter Orlovsky in an interview with James McKenzie in 1975, as well as in Barry Gifford and Lawrence Lee, eds., *Jack's Book* (New York: St. Martin's Press, 1978), Neeli Cherkovsky's *Ferlinghetti: A Biography* (Garden City, N. Y.: Doubleday, 1979), and Michael McClure's *Scratching the Beat Surface* (San Francisco: North Point Press, 1882). The next five paragraphs incorporate quotations from these sources into my own running commentary.

31. One of these is reproduced in Miles, *Howl: Original Draft Facsimile,* 165.

32. McClure, *Scratching the Beat Surface* 15, 21, with the text of the poem intevening. These comments are not reprinted in *Howl: Original Draft Facsimile.*

33. Miles, *Howl: Original Draft Facsimile,* 167.

34. Tom Clark, *Jack Kerouac* (San Diego: Harcourt, Brace, Jovanovich, 1984), 140, 147, 149. Clark's long familiarity with the San Francisco scene makes his accounts of contretemps there the best reading out of numerous books about Kerouac.

35. Ibid., 140, Allen Ginsberg as quoted Gifford and Lee, *Jack's Book,* 198.

36. When frequency modulation (FM), which had been developed during World War II for military use, was made available to the public, "good music" stations, like Washington, D.C.'s WGMS, sprang up in major cities and especially on college campuses to increase the fitful and noisy supply of classical music and radio drama. Pacifica Radio, which eventually expanded to Los Angeles and New York, was distinguished by its intelligent forums on controversial issues and its poetry readings.

37. A revised typescript of the poem appears in Charters, *The Beats,* 198.

38. The courteous and judicious Parkinson himself was shortly to have sad reason to know how much the environment of the once genteel area had changed when, during the free speech movement and other turbulent events on the Berkeley campus during the 1960s, he was shot at, his face and neck pocked with bird shot, and his graduate assistant was killed in his office by "a poor lunatic" who thought that because Parkinson sympathized with the student protesters he was a communist. See John R. Cooley's essay on Parkinson in *Contemporary Poets,* 4th ed., eds. James Vinson and Daniel Kirkpatrick (London and Chicago: St. James Press, 1985), 648.

39. Mark Andrew Johnson, *Robert Duncan* (Boston: Twayne, 1988), 5.

40. Michael Davidson, "Jack Spicer," in Charters, *The Beats,* 511.

41. Robert Stock, "Letter from San Francisco," *Poetry Broadside,* no. 2 (Summer 1957), 3, 13–14. Indexes to little magazines during the late 1950s list further letters from San Francisco by Stock in subsequent issues of *Poetry Broadside,* but I have not been able to locate copies of these issues. If they can be found, they would provide a unique account of the tense atmosphere created by rival groups of poets during these years of great activity.

42. Lawrence Ferlinghetti, "Horn on *Howl,*" *Evergreen Review,* no. 4 (1957), 145–58. Unless otherwise noted, all details and quotations in the next six paragraphs are from this article.

43. Quoted in *The Reporter* (12 December 1957), reprinted in David Perlman, "How Captain Hanrahan Made *Howl* a Best-Seller," in Miles, *Howl: Original Draft Facsimile,* 171. Appendix 3 also contains excerpts from Ferlinghetti's "Horn on *Howl,*" Shigeyoshi Murao's "Footnotes to My Arrest for Selling *Howl,*" and a more complete text of Judge Horn's decision than Ferlinghetti supplies in "Horn on *Howl.*"

44. Anne Waldman, "Interview with Philip Whalen," *The Beat Diary,* 85.

45. Reprinted in *The Beat Road,* 35.

46. James McKenzie, "An Interview with Allen Ginsberg," *The Beat Journey (unspeakable visions of the individual* 8) (1978), 9.

Chapter Two

1. Clark, *Jack Kerouac,* 164.

2. See Warren French, *Jack Kerouac* (Boston: Twayne, 1986), 33–45, for an analysis of the misreadings of *On the Road,* and 51–55, for an account of the prophesying of "the great rucksack revolution" in *The Dharma Bums.*

3. Rexroth, "Disengagement," 40–41.

4. "To the Reader," *New World Writing* 15 (June 1959), iii.

5. Mark Schorer, "On Lady Chatterley's Lover," *Evergreen Review,* no. 1 (1957), 161.

6. Rexroth, "San Francisco Letter," *Evergreen Review,* no. 2 (1957), 5–6, 13.

7. Clark, *Jack Kerouac,* 154.

8. Allen Ginsberg, "Siesta in Xbalba and Return to the States," *Evergreen Review,* no. 4 (1957), 46.

9. Louis Simpson, "Poets in Isolation," *Hudson Review* 9 (Autumn 1957), 464.

10. Simpson, "Orpheus in America," ibid., 375.

11. Benjamin Demott, "Cozzens and Others," *Hudson Review* 9 (Winter 1957), 620.

12. Gene Frumkin, "A Squawk about 'Squeal,' " *Coastlines,* no. 9 (Winter 1957–58), 47–48.

13. I am following the meticulously edited text of Parkinson, *A Casebook on the Beat,* 201–12, but page references in this text follow the original pagination of the article, "The Know-Nothing Bohemians," *Partisan Review* 25 (Spring 1958), 305–18. The article also appears in Seymour Krim, ed., *The Beats,* 11–24, and in *The Beats: An Anthology of Beat Writing,* ed. Park Honan (London: J. M. Dent & Sons, 1987), 216–29, among other places.

14. Leroi Jones, "Correspondence: The Beat Generation," *Partisan Review* 25 (Summer 1958), 472–73.

15. Diana Trilling, "The Other Night at Columbia," *Partisan Review* 26 (Spring 1959), 214–30.

16. "Diana Tilling" (Robert Bly), "The Other Night in Heaven," *The Fifties*, 3d issue (1959), 56.

17. "Crunk" (Robert Bly), "The Work of Robert Creeley," *The Fifties*, 2d issue (1959), 21, 12.

18. "Crunk" (Robert Bly), "The Work of Gary Snyder," *The Sixties*, no. 6 (Spring 1962), 36.

19. Again, I am following Parkinson's text in *A Casebook on the Beat*, 257–65, which provides the original pagination for John Ciardi, "Epitaph for the Dead Beats," *Saturday Review* (6 February 1960), 11–13, 42.

20. Michael Renner, "Ginsberg among the Hindus," *Graduate Student Journal* 3 (Spring 1964), 5. This journal was published by the Graduate Students Association of the University of California at Berkeley, where Renner was a graduate student in political science.

21. Ibid., 18.

22. Ciardi, "Epitaph," 13.

23. Jack Kerouac, "The Wheel of the Quivering Meat Conception," *Chicago Review* 12 (Spring 1958): 5 (hereafter cited in the text). Kerouac's intimations of death are especially depressing as the cries of a talented man who never learned how to live.

24. "Squaresville U.S.A. vs. Beatsville," *Life*, 21 September 1959, 31.

25. Bruce E. Hunsberger, letter to the editor, *Life*, 12 October 1959.

26. Again, I am following Parkinson's text in *A Casebook on the Beat*, 232–46, which provides the original pagination for Paul O'Neil, "The Only Rebellion Around," *Life*, 30 November 1959, 115–30.

27. Howard Thompson, "The Beat Generation," *New York Times*, 22 October 1959, 47.

28. Alix Kates Shulman, "The Beat Queens: Boho Chicks Stand by Their Men," [*Village*] *Voice Literary Supplement*, no. 75, June 1989, 18–23.

29. Maura Devereux, "Allen Ginsberg," *Boulder* [Colorado] *Sunday Camera Magazine*, 30 July 1989, 7.

30. Feldman and Gartenberg, *The Beat Generation*, 12.

31. Ibid., 20.

32. Quoted in Samuel Charters, "Chandler Brossard," in Charters, *The Beats*, 44.

33. Joseph Wenke, "Seymour Krim," in Charters, *The Beats*, 317.

34. Krim, *The Beats*, 10.

35. Ibid., 60.

36. Barbara Moraff, "Tune," *Evergreen Review*, no. 10 (November–December 1959), 47.

37. Allen Ginsberg, "Notes written on Finally Recording *Howl*," ibid., 133.

38. Allen Ginsberg, "Sather Gate Illumination," *Evergreen Review,* no. 11 (January–February 1960), 99. The poem also appears in Allen Ginsberg, *Collected Poems* (New York: Harper & Row, 1984), 145.

39. Donald M. Allen, *The New American Poetry: 1945–1960* (New York: Grove Press, 1960), hereafter cited in the text.

40. The confusing five-part arrangement was abandoned in Donald M. Allen and George F. Butterick, eds., *The Postmoderns: The New American Poetry Revised* (New York: Grove Press, 1982) and the poets are introduced in the chronological order of their birthdates from Charles Olson to Anne Waldman. Diane Di Prima is also included, but Orlovsky, Perkoff, Bremser, Loewinsohn, and Sorrentino have been dropped. This new edition provides a less varied introduction to beat writing than the *Beatitude Anthology.*

41. "Beatitude," *Beatitude Anthology,* [3].

42. "Private Eye's Undercover Job in Beatnik Dope Ring Lauded," *San Francisco Chronicle,* 23 January 1960, 1.

43. "Big Beatnik Rally to Protest Raids," *San Francisco Sunday Chronicle,* 31 January 1960, 1, 5.

44. Ralph Tyler, "Beatniks to Investigate Private Lives of Police," *San Francisco Sunday Chronicle,* 7 February 1960, 26.

45. "Wailing Wall," *Beatitude Anthology,* 88.

46. Jory Sherman from San Francisco, letter to the author, 24 April 1960.

47. Jory Sherman from San Francisco, letter to the author, 29 April 1960. He comments that Ruth Weiss, another regular contributor to *Beatitude,* "is the only one here who reads [i.e., gives public readings from her work] more than I do. . . . She is really a promoter and gets out on the streets and sells her books like mad."

48. "San Francisco Supplement," *Gemini* (Summer 1960), 35. The reporter added, "Beatniks are hard to find. Most of them have left for New York or Venice West." Whoever this was, was not too familiar with the beat scene; Richard Gumbiner, for instance, was as identified "Richard Gumbinder, a contributor to *Beatitudes.*"

49. Kenneth Rexroth, "The Commercialization of the Image of Revolt," reprinted in Charters, *The Beats,* 649.

50. Dean Lipton, "The Last Days of the Co-Existence Bagel Shop," *Cavalier* (November 1963), 37. Jory Sherman in his April letters quoted above also mentions the threat Mad Marie posed to the tranquillity of the community.

51. Philip Whalen, *Scenes of Life at the Capital* (Bolinas, Calif.: Grey Fox Press, 1971), 34.

Chapter Three

1. Jack Kerouac, *On the Road: Text and Criticism,* ed. Scott Donaldson (New York: Viking Press/Penguin, 1979), 18; hereafter cited in the text.

2. Rexroth, "Disengagement," 41.

3. John Clellon Holmes, "The Philosophy of the Beat Generation," *Esquire* (1958), reprinted in Charters, *The Beats,* 635–36.

4. The beats' affinities with Thoreau have been less noted than those with Whitman but are discussed in Tom Korson's "Duluoz, Thoreau, and the Artist's Ideal in *Desolation Angels*," *Kerouac Connection,* no. 12 (November 1986), 3–4.

5. Whalen, *Scenes of Life at the Capital,* 10, 40.

6. The difference brought into focus by different presentations of these two masterpieces, both of which teeter misunderstood on the brink of great watersheds in the eras of their respective sensibilities, is that between what are usually labeled the "classic" and "romantic" tempers in cultural history. The distinction is lucidly explained by Jacques Barzun in *Classic, Romantic, and Modern* (New York: Doubleday/Anchor Books, 1961); he contrasts Descartes' *Discourse-on Method* with Goethe's *Faust:* "The lesson of Descartes can presumably be learned from reading the remainder of [his book]. Descartes has done the perilous work; he has taken the risks and wrested the true answers from his experience. The lesson that Faust learns can only be found in the undergoing of the experience itself" (87–88).

7. *Beatitude Anthology,* 7; hereafter cited in the text.

8. Marilyn Schwartz, "Gregory Corso," in Charters, *The Beats,* 118.

9. Carolyn Gaiser, "Gregory Corso: A Poet, the Beat Way," in Parkinson, *A Casebook on the Beat,* 271. The first book-length critique of Corso is Gregory Stephenson's *Exiled Angel* (London: Hearing Eye Press, 1989).

10. McClure, *Scratching the Beat Surface,* 5, 10.

11. Steve Dossey and Donna Wood, "An Interview with Pierre DeLattre," *Beat Angels (unspeakable visions of the individual,* no. 12) (1982), 75.

12. "Minister for the Beatniks: Bread and Wine Mission," *Newsweek,* 16 March 1959, 88; Irving Feldman, "Far-Out Mission: Bread and Wine Mission," *Time,* 29 June 1959, 38.

13. Dossey and Wood, 75.

14. Jack Kerouac, *Big Sur* (New York: Farrar, Straus and Cudahy, 1962), 172.

15. Quoted in Donna Nance, "Lenore Kandel," Charters, *The Beats,* 272.

16. The correspondence in which this speculation occurs—following a description of Ferlinghetti's work as "a nonsensical, difficult to understand, dissertation"—is reprinted in "Letters from the FBI," *City Lights Journal,* no. 4 (1978), 236, as part of a collection of documents obtained under the Freedom of Information Act.

17. Kerouac, *Vanity of Duluoz,* 85. Kerouac's distaste for anything political became mordant. Early in this novel he writes of Americans' being "eviscerated of 1930's innocent ambition" by World War II (15).

18. A. D. Winans, "Bob Kaufman," in Charters, *The Beats,* 277.

Chapter Four

1. Quoted in Lawrence Ferlinghetti, "Horn on *Howl*," *Evergreen Review*, No. 4 (1957), 152.

2. See Introduction, note 2.

3. Allen, *New American Poetry*, 420. Both Whalen's poeticized statements of his position and his prosaic ones indicate how far the beats were from being, as John Ciardi charged, "an essentially adolescent rebellion . . . marked by an orthodoxy as rigid as the blue laws" ("Epitaph for the Dead Beats," 11), although the charge was frequently leveled by critics and makers of trashy movies.

4. See Chapter 3, note 7, for Jacques Barzun's explanation of the romantic view of experience illustrated by Whitman's lines.

5. Whalen, *Scenes of Life at the Capital*, 9.

6. Ibid., 43

7. Allen, *New American Poetry*, 420.

8. Anne Waldman, "An Interview with Philip Whalen," *The Beat Diary*, 83. The specific questions mentioned were posed by Lewis Warsh; also present were Michael Brownstein, Tom Clark, and Lewis MacAdams. In this long interview in Bolinas, California, in September 1971, about the time of the publication of *Scenes of Life at the Capital*, Whalen discusses not only his lifestyle and poetry but the two novels he had published—*You Didn't Even Try* (1967) and *Imaginary Speeches for a Brazen Head* (1972)—which are beyond the scope of this study. A detailed account of Whalen's poetry by Paul Christensen appears in Charters, *The Beats*, 554–72.

9. *Evergreen Review*, no. 10 (November–December 1959), 47, and no. 24 (May–June 1962), 72.

10. Anne Waldman, "An Interview with Diane Di Prima," *The Beat Road*, 31. Moraff is the only one of the women on the San Francisco scene in the 1950s whose whereabouts Di Prima then knew. Moraff is not included in Ann Charters's *The Beats*.

11. Editor's note, *The Miscellaneous Man* 1 (April 1954), 1.

12. Lilith Lorraine, "Daylight Saving," ibid., 10.

13. Robert Hawley and Ann Charters, "David Meltzer," in Charters, *The Beats*, 405–10.

14. Mentioning that Robert Stock holds get-togethers for poets at his home every week (in the Rexroth tradition), Jory Sherman observed that "Bob is too traditional for me to take all evening" (letter to the author, 29 April 1960).

15. I have not been able to locate further information about Richardson, but Jory Sherman mentioned in 1960 that his friend Richardson was "another Negro poet here," who was staying with Robert Stock (letter to the author, 23 April 1960).

16. The copy in the Harris Collection at the John Hay Library, Brown University, contains an autographed inscription to another graduating classmate.

17. David Rafael Wang, *The Intercourse* (Greenfield Center, N.Y.: Greenfield Review Press, 1975); hereafter cited in text.

18. David Rafael Wang, "The Grandfather Cycle," *Poetry Broadside,* no. 2 (Summer 1957), 4–5.

19. Wand, David Happel Hsin-Fu, *Asian-American Heritage* (New York: Washington Square Press, 1974), 4.

20. For details of Brautigan's years among the beats before he turned from poetry to prose fiction, see Edward Halsey Foster, *Richard Brautigan* (Boston: Twayne, 1983).

Chapter Five

1. Michael McClure's *Scratching the Beat Surface* (1982) is indeed just that, for it scratches up only the most significant events of the poetry renaissance years. It is to be hoped that such a charming writer will yet provide fuller reminiscences of that time.

2. Lawrence Lipton, *The Holy Barbarians* (New York: Julian Messner, 1959; Black Cat ed., 1962, New York: Grove Press), 15–16; hereafter cited in text. Venice West has still not shared in its region's general prosperity but remains a rundown and antiquated resort, where social outcasts of varying persuasions continue to seek asylum.

3. The principal Los Angeles contribution to the avant-garde during the 1950s was James Boyer May's monthly *Trace,* a periodical essential to the history of small press publishing during those years; it provided information about the founding and folding of little magazines and a forum for the exchange of information between editors and often outraged poets, along with occasional poems and stories.

4. William Hogan, "A Few Cool Words for *Howl,*" *San Francisco Chronicle,* May 1957, reprinted in *Coastlines,* no. 8 (Autumn 1957), 34.

5. Lawrence Lipton, "I Was a Poet for the FBI," *Coastlines,* no. 9 (Winter 1957–58), 6.

6. Blunderbuss Column, "Barbarians to and from the North," ibid., 44.

7. Gene Frumkin, "A Squawk about 'Squeal' " (editorial), ibid., 47–48. A special issue of *Epos* was devoted to promoting Los Angeles poetry. Will Tullos and Evelyn Thorne's long-running Florida quarterly contained works of twenty-six poets and linoleum cuts by Polia Pillin, selected by William Pillin, who argued in a prefatory statement that "the poets of Los Angeles are moved by the same psychic motivations as the poets of San Francisco, but perhaps in a manner less calculated to provoke a journalistic sensation." A more bizarre and distant effort to promote the group were two issues in 1956 and 1957 of Harry Hooton's *21st. Century* in Sydney, Australia. Lawrence Lipton was a contributor, along with Leslie Woolf Hedley, James Boyer May, and others. Each of the thousand copies of the second issue was bound in "a share of the largest painting in the world," an abstract work that was cut up for this purpose.

8. Nettie Lipton, "Lawrence Lipton," in Charters, *The Beats,* 355.

9. Donald Pease, *Visionary Compacts: American Renaissance Writings in Cultural Context* (Madison: University of Wisconsin Press, 1987). Pease's book is an attempt to update F. O. Matthiessen's concept of an "American Renaissance" by, among other things, substituting Edgar Allan Poe for Thoreau in the original pantheon of five writers. Pease mentions Thoreau only condescendingly on a very few occasions in this critical study, which is distinctly not beat-oriented.

10. Lipton was not alone in fomenting confusion. When the *Beloit Poetry Journal,* one of the most respected academic little magazines, used its Winter 1957–58 issue to foreshadow Gene Feldman and Max Gartenberg's linking of an American "Underground" with the British "Movement," no San Franciscans were represented in the group selected by James Boyer May. Included instead were almost exclusively Los Angeles-connected poets—Gil Orlovitz, Leslie Woolf Hedley, and Charles Bukowski, as well as the mysterious Judson Crews. William J. Margolis was included, but there was no mention at all of the Beat Generation.

11. Jaffe and Six's *Without Memorial Banners,* a tribute to the memory of Charlie "Bird" Parker, attracted nothing like the attention accorded to efforts to produce a rock opera, like the Who's *Tommy.*

12. Information about fashions in popular music comes from Lois and Alan Gordon, *American Chronicle: Six Decades in American Life 1920–1980* (New York: Atheneum, 1987), an invaluable year-by-year account of highlights of American popular and elite culture.

13. Sanford Dobrin, *A Bibliography of Charles Bukowski* (Los Angeles: Black Sparrow Press, 1969), 15. The edition was limited to two hundred copies, but Griffith still had some on hand as late as 1965.

14. David Rafael Wang, " 'Beauty Is So Rare,' " *Hearse,* no. 5 (undated), 8.

15. Leroi Jones, "The Last Roundup," ibid., 15.

16. John Barkley Hart, "The Flight of Mr. Sun," ibid., 9, 11.

17. Diane Di Prima, "When Jeannie Wakes," *Hearse* no. 7 (undated), [14].

18. Warren French, "Diary of Anatole Tarsh," ibid., 16.

19. Charles Bukowski, "I Am Visited By An Editor And A Poet" (capitalized as printed), ibid., 7. Jory Sherman in a letter to the author, 29 April 1960, writes that Leslie Woolf Hedley, referred to in this poem, has become "almost a fanatic about beatniks."

20. Joseph Lanz made a quixotic effort to force San Francisco back into avant-garde leadership in 1984 when he dedicated his *Journal of Paranoia* in "Homage to Polystyrene: Reflections on Barbie and Ken's Twenty-fifth Anniversary" to the famous dolls as parodies of American "sexual phobias and obsessions"; but the failure of his project shows that the nation was no more ready for self-confrontation then than in Gershon Legman's heyday.

Chapter Six

1. "By 1970 it's quite possible that all books except deluxe editions will be in paperback form," Ferlinghetti predicted to Luther Nichols, book editor of the

San Francisco Examiner, for the paper's Sunday "Highlight" feature, 24 April 1960, 7.

2. Quoted in Devereux, "Allen Ginsberg," 7.

3. For details of this episode, see William R. King, "Michael McClure," Charters, *The Beats,* 391–93.

4. Jerry Tallmer, "Introduction," *Pull My Daisy* (New York: Grove Press, 1961), 18; hereafter cited in the text.

5. Jeffrey Grossman, "Acknowledgments," *Beatitude* 33 (1985); hereafter cited in the text.

6. E. L. Borenstein, "Jazz in New Orleans: 1957 to 1963," *The Outsider,* no. 3 (Spring 1963), 117.

7. Howard Nemerov, "The Iron Characters," *The Outsider,* no. 2 (Summer 1972), 13.

8. Thomas F. Merrill, *Allen Ginsberg,* rev. ed. (Boston: Twayne, 1988), 111; hereafter cited in the text.

9. Naropa Institute, 1988–1990 Catalog, 8.

10. James McKenzie, " 'I'm Poor Simple Human Bones': An Interview with Gregory Corso," *The Beat Diary,* 4.

11. Ann Charters, "Anne Waldman" in Charters, *The Beats,* 528. Most of the information about Waldman's background comes from "My Life List" in *Talking Poetics from Naropa Institute,* ed. Anne Waldman (Boulder: Shambhala Publications, 1979); hereafter cited in the text.

12. *Naropa Institute,* 1988–1990 Catalog, 76.

13. The documents connected with this genuinely distressing episode, which has no connection with the beats as a group, are reprinted in a narrative account by Tom Clark, *The Great Naropa Poetry Wars* (Santa Barbara; Calif.: Cadmus Editions, 1980). Clark, who was writer for the *Boulder Monthly* and was especially outraged by the affair and his treatment as a reporter, is highly critical of Trungpa and Ginsberg. Ginsberg does not appear to best advantage in the transcript offered here of his interview with Clark in February 1979, particularly in his remarks about "people who suck up to Castro and Mao Tse-Tung . . . or who put up with Leroi Jones" (65).

14. Ron Dart, in a report from the *Los Angeles Times,* reprinted in *Washington Post,* 8 April 1989, C-13.

15. Linda Cornett, "Naropa Plans $3 Million Expansion," *Boulder* (Colorado) *Sunday Camera,* 31 July 1988, 5-A; Margie McAllister, "New Mental Health Program Set," *Boulder Daily Camera,* 1 August 1988, 1-C.

16. Allen Ginsberg, postcard to the author, 3 August 1989.

17. I was struck that as I was finishing the typescript for this book on 17 October 1989, the day that the worst earthquake since 1906 struck the San Francisco Bay Area, particularly the Marina District, where the poetry renaissance originated in 1955, Barry Norman's "Film 89" program on BBC-TV reported that Peter

Weir's *Dead Poets Society,* the first film I know to truly embody the beat sensibility, was the top-drawing film that week at England's cinemas.

18. Kingsley Widmer, "The Beat in the Rise of Populist Culture," *The Fifties: Fiction, Poetry, Drama,* ed. Warren French (Deland, Fla.: Everett/Edwards, 1970); hereafter cited in the text.

Selected Bibliography

PRIMARY WORKS

Anthologies/Collections

Most of these anthologies also contain bibliographies.

Allen, Donald M., ed. *The New American Poetry, 1945–1960*. New York: Grove Press, 1960. Although Allen's classification of San Francisco poets is confusing, this remains the trail-blazing guide to the "nonacademic" poetry of the interrelated Black Mountain, New York, and San Francisco schools; see Chapter 2.

Ferlinghetti, Lawrence, ed. *Beatitude Anthology*. San Francisco: City Lights Books, 1960. This 111-page collection of some seventy-five poems, three prose pieces, and a letter selected from the first fifteen issues of *Beatitude* is the most important treasury of the San Francisco Poetry Renaissance; its contents are analyzed in Chapters 3 and 4.

Fisher, Stanley, ed. *Beat Coast East: An Anthology of Rebellion*. New York: Excelsior Press, 1960. Not many San Franciscans are included, but this ninety-six-page assemblage of poetry, prose, and drawings presents a panoramic view of beat writing in Greenwich Village.

Honan, Park, ed. *The Beats: An Anthology of "Beat" Writing*. London: J. M. Dent and Sons, 1987. An introduction by an American-born scholar who teaches in England for a new generation of interested readers abroad; it also contains some criticism and a bibliography.

Knight, Arthur Winfield, and Glee Knight, eds. *The Beat Book*. California, Pa.: tuvoti, 1974. Volume 4 of a series of publications in various forms, begun in 1971, under the general title, *the unspeakable visions of the indidual,* this was the first collection of essays to deal exclusively with the beats and the last to be coedited by Glee Knight before her death. It includes material by Philip Whalen, Michael McClure, Jack Micheline, Bob Kaufman, and Lawrence Ferlinghetti, among others. The series was continued by Arthur and Kit Knight (see below).

Knight, Arthur Winfield, and Kit Knight, eds. *the unspeakable visions of the individual*. California, Pa.: tuvoti, 1977–85. An incredible devotional effort consisting of ten major publications in various forms—ranging from reproductions of broadsides to two-hundred-page collections of letters, memoirs, interviews with beat writers, previously unpublished works, and many photographs—as well as smaller pieces. The most important collections are *The Beat Diary* (vol. 5, 1977), *The Beat Journey* (vol. 8, 1978), the tenth anniversary issue, (vol. 10, 1980), *Beat Angels* (vol. 12, 1982), and *The Beat Road* (vol. 14, 1984). Selections have been collected in *The Beat Vision* and in *Kerouac and the Beats* (New York: Paragon House, 1988). Arthur Knight has published a history of this unique venture, "*the unspeakable visions of the individual:* A History," *Kerouac Connection,* nos. 11 and 12 (July and November 1986).

McDarrah, Fred W. *Kerouac and Friends: A Beat Generation Album.* New York: William Morrow, 1985. A very useful book by the celebrated photographer of Greenwich Village life. Besides many informal pictures, it also includes thirty articles by and about the beats, many reprints of hard-to-find pieces from the 1950s and 1960s, as well as biographical sketches and a detailed bibliography.

Meltzer, David. *The San Francisco Poets.* New York: Ballantine Books, 1971; reissued in altered form as *Golden Gate: Interviews with Five San Francisco Poets,* Berkeley, Calif.: Wingbow Press, 1976. Long interviews with Richard Brautigan, William Everson, Lawrence Ferlinghetti, Michael McClure, Kenneth Rexroth, and Lew Welch that contain little about the poetry renaissance but much background detail about literary life in the city. For unexplained reasons, the Brautigan interview is omitted from the reissue.

Parkinson, Thomas, ed. *A Casebook on the Beat.* New York: Thomas Y. Crowell, 1961. Part of a series designed to provide materials for undergraduate college research papers, this is the most complete and authentic portrait of the poetry renaissance just as it was ending, as closely observed by this poet and University of California professor. Besides poetry and prose by nine writers, it includes important criticisms, one by the editor, and the most comprehensive bibliography of writings about the poetry renaissance while it was in progress.

"San Francisco Scene," *Evergreen Review* 1, no. 2 (1957). The collection of poetry and prose by seventeen writers—not all beats—with an introductory letter by Kenneth Rexroth, that first introduced most of these writers to a national audience.

Chapbooks and Related Collections

Only titles printed during the poetry renaissance, or later collections containing works written during that period by contributors to *Beatitude* and those closely associated with them, are included, arranged chronologically. For more bibliographic information on some writers, see *The Beats,* ed. Ann Charters. Unless otherwise specified, all titles are small chapbooks or collections of poems by one or several authors.

It is noteworthy that most chapbooks did not appear until after *Beatitude* began publication during the last months of the poetry renaissance. The beat/beatnik period in North Beach was disproportionately short—less than a year—in view of the long-term effects that it has had on American culture.

Corso, Gregory. *The Vestal Lady on Brattle and Other Poems*. Cambridge, Mass.: Richard Bruckenfeld, 1955.

————. *Gasoline*. San Francisco: City Lights Books, 1958.

————. *Bomb* (broadside). San Francisco: City Lights Books, 1958.

————. *The Happy Birthday of Death*. New York: New Directions, 1960.

Ferlinghetti, Lawrence. *Pictures of the Gone World*. San Francisco: City Lights Books (Pocket Poet Series, no. 1), 1955.

————. *A Coney Island of the Mind*. Norfolk, Conn.: New Directions, 1958; enlarged edition, New York: New Directions, 1968.

————. *Tentative Description of a Dinner Given to Promote the Impeachment of President Eisenhower* (broadside). San Francisco: City Lights Books, 1958.

————. *Her* (novel). Norfolk, Conn.: New Directions, 1960.

————. *Starting from San Francisco*. Norfolk, Conn.: New Directions, 1961.

Ginsberg, Allen. *Howl and Other Poems*. San Francisco: City Lights Books, 1956.

————. *Kaddish and Other Poems: 1958–1960*. San Francisco: City Lights Books, 1961.

————. *Reality Sandwiches: 1953–1960*. San Francisco: City Lights Books, 1963.

————. *Collected Poems: 1947–1980*. New York: Harper & Row, 1984.

————. *Howl: Original Draft Facsimile, Transcript and Variant Versions, Fully Annotated by Author, with Contemporaneous Correspondence, Account of First Public Reading, Legal Skirmishes, Precursor Texts, and Bibliography*, ed. Barry Miles. New York: Harper & Row, 1986.

Hitchcock, George. *The Wounded Alphabet: Poems 1953–1983*. Santa Cruz, Calif.: Jazz Press/Papa Bach, 1983.

————, with Mel Fowler. *Poems and Prints*. San Francisco: San Francisco Review, 1962.

Kaufman, Bob. *The Abomunist Manifesto* (broadside, satirical prose). San Francisco: City Lights Books, 1959.

————. *Second April* (broadside). San Francisco: City Lights Books, 1959.

————. *Does the Secret Mind Whisper?* (broadside). San Francisco: City Lights Books, 1960.

————. *Solitudes Crowded with Loneliness*. New York: New Directions, 1965.

Kerouac, Jack. *On the Road* (novel). New York: Viking Press, 1957.

————. *The Dharma Bums* (novel). New York: Viking Press, 1958.

————. *The Subterraneans*. New York: Grove Press, 1958.

————. *Mexico City Blues*. New York: Grove Press, 1959.

————. *Rimbaud* (broadside). San Francisco: City Lights Books, 1960.

————. *Lonesome Traveler* (essays). New York: McGraw-Hill, 1960.

————. *Pull My Daisy* (overvoice narration for Robert Frank's film, with stills from the film). New York: Grove Press, 1961.

————. *Book of Dreams* (memoirs). San Francisco: City Lights Books, 1961.

————. *Big Sur* (autobiographical novel). New York: Farrar, Straus and Cudahy, 1962.

Lamantia, Philip. *Ekstasis*. San Francisco: Auerhahn Press, 1959.

————, with Charles Bukowski and Harold Norse. *Penguin Modern Poets* 13. Harmondsworth, Eng.: Penguin Books, 1969.

MacLaine, Christopher. *The Time Capsule*. San Francisco: 16 Adler Press, 1960.

Margolis, William J. *The Anteroom of Hell*. San Francisco: Inferno Press, 1957.

Marshall, Edward. *Hellan. Hellan*. San Francisco: Auerhahn Press, 1960.

McBride, Richard. *Oranges* with illustrations by Victor Wong. San Francisco: Bread and Wine Press, 1960.

McClure, Michael. *Passage*. Big Sur: Jonathan Williams, 1956.

————. *For Artaud*. New York: Totem Press, 1959.

————. *Hymns to St. Geryon and Other Poems*. San Francisco: Auerhahn Press, 1959.

————. *The New Book: A Book of Torture*. New York: Grove Press, 1961.

————. *Scratching the Beat Surface* (essays and memoirs). San Francisco: North Point Press, 1982.

Meltzer, David. *Ragas: Poems*. San Francisco: Discovery Books, 1959.

Orlovsky, Peter. *Dear Allen: Ship will land Jan 23 58*. Buffalo: Intrepid Press, 1971.

Reed, Blake. *21 Carlisle*. San Francisco: Bread and Wine Press, 1960.

Sherman, Jory. *So Many Rooms*. San Francisco: Galley Sail Publications, 1960.

Snyder, Gary. *Riprap*. Ashland, Mass.: Origin Press, 1959.

————. *Myths and Texts*. New York: Totem Press/Corinth Books, 1960.

Uronowitz, Berne A. *Reflections in the Dark, Instant Poems*. New Rochelle, N.Y.: Elizabeth Press, 1961.

Wang, David Rafael. *The Intercourse*. Greenfield Center, N.Y.: Greenfield Review Press, 1975.

Weiss, Ruth. *South Pacific*. San Francisco: Adler Press, 1959.

Welch, Lew. *Wobbly Rock*. San Francisco: Auerhahn Press, 1960.

————, with Jack Kerouac and Albert Saijo. *Trip Trap: Haiku along the Road from San Francisco to New York*. Bolinas, Calif.: Grey Fox Press, 1973.

Whalen, Philip. *Self-Portrait from Another Direction*. San Francisco: Auerhahn Press, 1960.

————. *Like I Say*. New York: Totem Press/Corinth Books, 1960.

————. *Memoirs of an Interglacial Age*. San Francisco: Auerhahn Press, 1959.

————. *On Bear's Head: Selected Poems*. New York: Harcourt, Brace & World, 1969.

Wieners, John. *The Hotel Wentley Poems*. San Francisco: Auerhahn Press, 1958.

Periodicals

Entries are limited to those principally supporting San Francisco Poetry Renaissance writers between 1956 and 1960 and to those directly continuing their tradition. For a fuller list of "beat-inspired" serials with illustrations, see George F. Butterick, "Periodicals of the Beat Generation," in *The Beats,* ed. Ann Charters, 651–88.

Ark II/Moby I (San Francisco, 1956), eds. James Harmon and Michael McClure.
Beatitude, nos. 1–15 (San Francisco, 1959–60), eds. John Kelly and others; no. 33 (San Francisco, 1985), ed. Jeffrey Grossman.
Big Table, nos. 1–5 (Chicago, 1959–60), ed. Paul Carroll.
Black Mountain Review, no. 7 (Black Mountain, N.C., Autumn 1957), ed. Robert Creeley, with Allen Ginsberg.
Chicago Review, vol. 11, no. 4, and vol. 12, nos. 1–3 (Chicago, 1958), ed. Irving Rosenthal.
City Lights (San Francisco, 1952–55), eds. Peter Martin and Lawrence Ferlinghetti.
City Lights Journal 1–4 (San Francisco, 1963–78), ed. Lawrence Ferlinghetti.
Evergreen Review, nos. 2–20 (New York, 1957–61), ed. Barney Rosset.
Floating Bear (New York, 1961–71), ed. Diane Di Prima.
The Hasty Papers (Binghamton, N. Y., 1960), ed. Alfred Leslie.
Hearse, nos. 1–9 (Eureka, Calif., 1957–61), ed. E. V. Griffith.
Journal for the Protection of All Beings, nos. 1–4 (San Francisco, 1961–78), eds. Lawrence Ferlinghetti, Michael McClure, David Meltzer, and Gary Snyder.
Miscellaneous Man, nos. 1–15 (Berkeley, Calif., 1954–59), ed. William J. Margolis.
Neon, nos. 1–15 (Brooklyn, N.Y., 1959–60), ed. Gilbert Sorrentino.
Neurotica, nos. 1–9 (St. Louis and New York, 1948–52), ed. Jay Irving Landesman.
The Outsider, nos. 1–3 (New Orleans, 1961–63), ed. Jon Edgar Webb.
Yugen, nos. 1–8 (New York, 1958–62), eds. LeRoi Jones and Hettie Cohen.

SECONDARY WORKS

Bibliography

Charters, Ann, ed. *The Beats: Literary Bohemians in Postwar America.* Dictionary of Literary Biography, vol. 16, in two parts. Detroit: Bruccoli Clark/ Gale Research, 1983. Although this mammoth compilation contains the most extensive bibliographies anywhere of books and periodicals by and about not only the general subject but sixty-eight individual writers, it is far more than a bibliography. It contains critical essays by various writers for each entry, as well as general essays on the Beat Generation and a twenty-five-year chronology by Jennie Skerl. The starting point for all studies of the postwar counterculture, though not all beats are included and not all of those included are beats. The subtitle best describes the whole.

Books

Bartlett, Lee, ed. *The Beats: Essays in Criticism.* Jefferson, N. C.: McFarland, 1981. The editor of *American Poetry,* and a longtime champion of the beats, brings together fourteen essays by John Clellon Holmes, Thomas Parkinson, William Everson, and distinguished critics. Emphasis is on Burroughs, Ginsberg, Kerouac, and Snyder, but also included are an essay on Bob Kaufman and Geoffrey Thurley's "The Development of a New Language: Michael McClure, Philip Whalen, and Gregory Corso."

Charters, Samuel. *Some Poems/Poets: Studies in American Underground Poetry since 1945.* Berkeley, Calif.: Oyez, 1971. Studies of Creeley and Duncan, as well as Ferlinghetti, Lew Welch, Brother Antoninus, and others at a time when attention was just returning to the beats, who had often been slighted during the activist years of the 1960s.

Cherkovski, Neeli. *Ferlinghetti: A Biography.* Garden City, N. Y.: Doubleday, 1979. Ferlinghetti's role as the principal promoter of the poetry renaissance makes his career central to an understanding of it and involves all the principal participants.

_____. *Whitman's Wild Children.* Venice, Calif. and San Francisco: Lapis Press, 1988. Impressions of the principal beats by a sympathetic writer closely involved with them.

Feldman, Gene and Max Gartenberg, eds. *The Beat Generation and the Angry Young Men.* New York: Citadel Press, 1958; reissued 1987, London: Souvenir Press. The first influential effort to take the beats seriously and link them with England's Angry Young Men, this book contains nothing connected with San Francisco Poetry Renaissance but *Howl.* Contents are carefully selected to focus on New York and London.

Horsmans, Rudi, ed. *Beat Indeed!* Antwerp, Belgium: Restant, 1985. A collection of largely unpublished materials that emphasizes Kerouac and the New York scene (John Clellon Holmes and Diane Di Prima). Although there is a study of Ferlinghetti, other studies cover Bukowski and Walker Percy's novel *The Moviegoer!*

Hyde, Lewis, ed. *On the Poetry of Allen Ginsberg.* Ann Arbor: University of Michigan Press 1989. Excellent collection of personal materials and critical essays, especially strong in material about *Howl* and the 1957 trial discussed in this book.

Kherdian, David. *Six Poets, of the San Francisco Renaissance: Portraits and Checklists* (Introduction by William Saroyan). Fresno, Calif.: Giligia Press, 1967. Avoids the more familiar figures treated in most critiques and provides biographical and bibliographical details about Ferlinghetti, Michael McClure, David Meltzer, Gary Snyder, and Philip Whalen, as well as William Everson (Brother Antoninus).

Krim, Seymour, ed. *The Beats.* Greenwich, Conn.: Gold Medal Books, 1960. A collection of then-unfamiliar pieces by Kerouac and Ginsberg, work by Diane Di Prima, Ray Bremser, Philip Lamantia, Jack Micheline, and Hubert Selby, Jr., as well as by Krim himself, and some favorable and unfavorable essays, linked together more usefully than in similar collections by Krim's running critique.

Lipton, Lawrence. *The Holy Barbarians.* New York: Julian Messner, 1959; Black Cat ed. 1962, New York: Grove Press. Though in part fictionalized, this "first complete inside story of the Beat Generation" is really a rambling essay—in the European tradition of bohemian anarchism—promoting "disaffiliation and the art of poverty" and jazz improvisation as the generation's music. Set in a rundown seaside suburb of Los Angeles, Venice West, it has misled many readers who take it for an account of the North Beach community in San Francisco in the late 1950s, with which it has little connection.

Saroyan, Aram. *Genesis Angels: The Saga of Lew Welch and the Beat Generation.* New York: William Morrow, 1979. Although he gives primarily an account of Welch's troubled life, Saroyan, by placing Welch against a broad social background, also provides a panoramic history of the beats from a different viewpoint than that most commonly provided by taking the meeting of Burroughs, Ginsberg, and Kerouac in New York as the starting point.

Stephenson, Gregory. *The Daybreak Boys: Essays on the Literature of the Beat Generation.* Carbondale: Southern Illinois University Press, 1990. A Danish critic collects his essays on principal writers—a fresh perspective.

————. *Exiled Angel: A Study of the Work of Gregory Corso.* London: Hearing Eye Press, 1989. The first book-length study of the writings of a poet slighted by many previous critics.

Tytell, John. *Naked Angels: The Lives and Literature of the Beat Generation.* New York: McGraw-Hill, 1976. The pioneering book to study the literary accomplishment of Burroughs, Ginsberg, and Kerouac against the social and political context of the times; excellent background reading for understanding the origins of the beats.

Weinberg, Jeffrey H., ed. *Writers Outside the Margin.* Sudbury, Mass.: Water Row Press, 1985. One of the most enterprising booksellers specializing in the beats is also adding to the canon. This melange of original works and criticisms is, as usual, heavy on Kerouac, but there are pieces about Corso and others by familiar writers on the beats.

Articles

Article-length contributions to Charters, Feldman and Gartenberg, Krim, and Parkinson are not included; they are discussed and identified in the text and notes.

Eberhart, Richard. "West Coast Rhythms: Richard Eberhart Discusses Group of Young Poets on West Coast." *New York Times Book Review,* 2 September 1956, 7. First enthusiastic report, by a distinguished academic poet, calling national attention to the North Beach community. Reprinted in Heyd.

Ferlinghetti, Lawrence. "Horn on *Howl.*" *Evergreen Review,* no.4 (1957), 145–58. Wry commentary on the accused in the *Howl* prosecution, with many quotations from the proceedings.

_____. "Note on Poetry in San Francisco." *Chicago Review* 12 (Spring 1958), 4. Strident call for "street poetry"; this article distinguishes Ferlinghetti's position from those of the beats whom he promoted and the "proletarian" writers of bombastic agitprop.

_____. "Letters from the FBI." *City Lights Journal,* no. 4 (1978), 233–40. Collection of ludicrous documents from FBI files on Ferlinghetti, Ginsberg, and Jane Fonda.

Glicksberg, Charles I. "Sex in Contemporary Literature." *Colorado Quarterly* 9 (Winter 1961), 277–87. A defense of the beat attitude toward sex as a mystical function that has extraordinary potential for human development.

Jones, Leroi. "Correspondence: The Beat Generation." *Partisan Review* 25 (Summer 1958), 472–73. Excerpts from a letter vigorously championing the beats against the pusillanimous attack in Norman Podhoretz's "The Know-Nothing Bohemians" (*Partisan Review* [Spring 1958]; reprinted everywhere as the New York establishment's position on the "wild beasts").

Lipton, Lawrence. "Disaffiliation and the Art of Poverty." *Chicago Review* 10 (Spring 1958), 53–79. Kernel of the doctrine of voluntary poverty to maintain artistic integrity developed in *The Holy Barbarians.*

Podell, Albert N. "Censorship on the Campus: The Case of the *Chicago Review.*" *San Francisco Review* 1 (1959), 71–89. Report on the University of Chicago administration's suppression of an issue of the *Chicago Review,* the action that led to the founding of *Big Table.*

Simpson, Louis. "Poets in Isolation." *Hudson Review* 9 (Autumn 1957), 458–64. A prominent academic poet includes in a lamentation about the state of poetry reviewing in the United States a snide parody of the beats as venal opportunitists; the parody backfired when it upset the beleaguered Los Angeles group supporting *Coastlines.*

Stock, Robert. "Letter from San Francisco." *Poetry Broadside,* no. 2 (Summer 1957), 3, 13–14. A jaundiced account by a highly traditional formal poet of the questionability of any renaissance in San Francisco.

Widmer, Kingsley. "The Beat in the Rise of Populist Culture." In *The Fifties: Fiction, Poetry, Drama,* ed. Warren French, 155–73. Deland, Fla.: Everett/

Edwards, 1970. Our outstanding scholar of American outsiders argues that while the beats have not produced a large body of significant literature, they have generated a broader revolution that continues to make great changes in American and international culture.

Wilson, Colin. "Some Comments on the Beats and Angries," *The Outsider,* no. 1 (Fall 1961), 57–60. The British subversive who gave the new magazine its name argues that so far the beat attitude has been largely a reaction and that the American beats must learn from Europe to value revolutionaries who have discipline and "a precision of mind."

Journals

The Kerouac Connection, ed. Dave Moore (19 Worthing Road, Patchway, Bristol, England BS12 5HY). Founded in 1984 as the newsletter of the British Beat Brotherhood, this quarterly has become an independent journal featuring articles, reminiscences, reviews, and news items concerning all those connected with or interested in the work of the Beat Generation; especially featured is the sizable British group, which is seldom discussed in the United States.

Moody Street Irregulars: A Jack Kerouac Newsletter, ed. Joy Walsh (P.O. Box 157, Clarence Center, N.Y. 14032). Despite the title, this journal—which has appeared about twice a year since it was founded in 1978—while especially devoted to Kerouac's memory, carries articles and reviews about all of the writers associated with the Beat Generation.

Index

Adam, Helen, 19
Agitprop, 99
Alcott, Bronson, 19
Allen, Donald M.: *The New American Poetry, 1945–1960*, 48–49, 73, 106, 119n40
Allen, Woody, 10, 115n24
Alpine, Texas, 74
American Civil Liberties Union (ACLU), 23
Amis, Sir Kingsley: *Lucky Jim*, 45
Amram, David, 97
Anderson, Chester V. J., 52, 53, 113n2
Anderson, Sherwood, 100
"Angry Young Men" (England, 1950's), 45–46, 90
Apollinaire, Guillaume, 85
Ark, The (San Francisco, 1947), 20
Arts and Crafts Movement (England, 19th Century), 37, 90
Ashbery, John, 40, 106
Ashton, Dore, 29
Atherton, Gertrude, 17
Auden, W. H., 34–35

Babbs, Ken, 109
"Ballad of Davy Crockett," 91
Band, The (rock group), 96
Baraka, Imamu Amiri, 109. *See also* Jones, Leroi
Barker, Richard, 47
Barzun, Jacques, 35, 40, 120n6
Baudelaire, Charles, 85
Beat frequency, xvii, 2, 96, 99
Beat Generation (defined), xvii, xx, 2, 6, 33, 41–43, 46–47, 55–58, 60, 68, 84, 121n3
Beat Generation, The (film) 20, 43, 44 (ill.)
Beat Hotel, Paris, 104
Beatitude, ix, x, xvii, 1–2, 13, 21, 45, 50–86, 99–100, 113n2
Beatitude Anthology, x, xviii, 2, 50–86

Beatles, The, 92
Beatniks (distinguished from beats), xix–xx, 8, 26, 36, 40–43, 52, 54, 56–57, 64, 68, 76–77, 90, 98, 113n3
Beckett, Samuel: *Waiting for Godot*, 48
Bendich, Albert, 23
Bennington College, 106
Berkeley Poetry Conference (1965), 107
Bigarini, William (San Francisco Police), 52
Big Sur, California, 10
Big Table (Chicago), 38–40
Black Mountain College (North Carolina), 14, 34–35, 48–49, 107
Black Mountain Review, 24–25
Blake, William, 105
Blaser, Robin, 30
Blavatsky, Madame Helen, 19
Bly, Robert, 34–35, 105
Borenstein, E. L., 101
Bougoureau, Adolphe, 4
Boyd, Bruce, 88
Braque, George, 5, 50
Brautigan, Richard, 50, 67, 84–85, 94
Bread and Wine Mission, xviii, 2, 63, 99
Breit, Harvey, 31
Breit, Luke, 99
Bremser, Ray, 47, 102, 109
Breton, André, 67
Brossard, Chandler, 2, 46–47
Brother Antoninus. *See* Everson, William
Broughton, James (filmmaker), 19, 29, 53
Brownstein, Michael, 109
Broyard, Anatole, 46–47
Buchwald, Art, 25
Buddhism, 12, 37, 64, 68, 100, 105–11
Bukowski, Charles, 11, 93–95, 102–103
Burgess, Gelett, 17
Burroughs, William, x, xvi, 6, 20, 25, 39, 43, 46, 47, 48, 97, 102, 105, 108, 109, 111

The Author

Warren French is an honorary professor of American studies at the University College of Swansea, Wales, a long way from his native Philadelphia. After graduating from the University of Pennsylvania, he first visited Europe with the U.S. Army in 1945. He did not get back to Europe until 1983, but since retiring from Indiana University in 1986, he spends most of his time traveling there. During the intervening decades, he acquired a Ph.D. at the University of Texas at Austin. After teaching at the Universities of Mississippi and Kentucky, he began collecting material for this book when he moved to the University of Florida in 1958, at the height of the beat years. While in Gainesville he also began his long association with the Twayne series with early books on John Steinbeck, Frank Norris, and J. D. Salinger. After being diverted to other projects during the 1960s at Kansas State University and the University of Missouri at Kansas City, he began spending his summers in Cornish Flat, New Hampshire. During this period, he rejoined Twayne to edit a filmmakers series, as well as the contemporary titles in the United States Authors Series, 1945–75. His most recent contributions to the series are *Jack Kerouac* and *J. D. Salinger, Revisited.* He is at work on a two-volume expansion of his critical biography of John Steinbeck during his annual visits to Ohio University in Athens, which honored him with a D. Litt. in 1985.